THE SOCIAL VENTURE NETWORK SERIES

mission, inc.

THE PRACTITIONER'S GUIDE TO SOCIAL ENTERPRISE

Kevin Ly

Julius Walls, Jr.

BK

Berrett–Koehler Publishers, Inc.
San Francisco

Berrett-Koehler Publishers, Inc.
235 Montgomery Street, Suite 650
San Francisco, CA 94104-2916
Tel: (415) 288-0260   Fax: (415) 362-2512   www.bkconnection.com

Ordering Information

Quantity sales. Special discounts are available on quantity purchases by corporations, associations, and others. For details, contact the "Special Sales Department" at the Berrett-Koehler address above.

Individual sales. Berrett-Koehler publications are available through most bookstores. They can also be ordered directly from Berrett-Koehler: Tel: (800) 929-2929; Fax: (802) 864-7626; www.bkconnection.com.

Orders for college textbook/course adoption use. Please contact Berrett-Koehler: Tel: (800) 929-2929; Fax: (802) 864-7626.

Orders by U.S. trade bookstores and wholesalers. Please contact Ingram Publisher Services: Tel: (800) 509-4887; Fax: (800) 838-1149; E-mail: customer.service@ingrampublisherservices.com; or visit www.ingrampublisher services.com/Ordering for details about electronic ordering.

Berrett-Koehler and the BK logo are registered trademarks of Berrett-Koehler Publishers, Inc.

Printed in the United States of America

Berrett-Koehler books are printed on long-lasting acid-free paper. When it is available, we choose paper that has been manufactured by environmentally responsible processes. These may include using trees grown in sustainable forests, incorporating recycled paper, minimizing chlorine in bleaching, or recycling the energy produced at the paper mill.

Library of Congress Cataloging-in-Publication Data
Lynch, Kevin.
  Mission, Inc. : a practitioner's guide to social enterprise / Kevin Lynch and Julius Walls, Jr.
  p. cm. — (Social venture network series)
  Includes bibliographical references and index.
  ISBN 978-1-57675-479-5 (pbk. : alk. paper)
    1. Entrepreneurship—Moral and ethical aspects. 2. Social entrepreneurship. 3. Social responsibility of business. 4. Industrial management—Moral and ethical aspects. 5. Quality of work life. I. Walls, Julius. II. Title. III. Title: Guide to social enterprise.
HB615.L96 2009
361.7068—dc22   2008041669

FIRST EDITION
14 13 12 11 10 09   10 9 8 7 6 5 4 3 2 1

Cover design by Crowfoot/Leslie Waltzer.

*For all those laborers of love who are
creating the common good*

Contents

Letter from the Editor of the
Social Venture Network Series

How many times have you seen or heard the phrase "social enterprise" during the past few years? A dozen? A hundred? A thousand? Through repeated overuse and misuse, this seemingly straightforward phrase has taken on a range of roles sufficient to overwhelm the most ambitious actor. What *you* mean when you use the phrase is probably not at all what *I* mean.

Now here come Kevin Lynch and Julius Walls, Jr., to toss out the playbill and present us with a broad, workable understanding of "social enterprise." In this brilliant little volume, they work from a definition that revolves around the purpose or mission of an enterprise (hence the title *Mission, Inc.*) rather than around its legal form or structure. Nonprofit, for-profit, cooperative, hybrid, whatever—it doesn't matter. What matters is the mission.

In Lynch and Walls's estimation, a social enterprise is a business that seeks, above all, to make the world a better place—a "business for the common good." This handy guideline, which eschews the hairsplitting definitions often bandied about at conferences and in books that promote one or another flavor of social enterprise, comes at a convenient time in the evolution of business. The lines between for-profit and not-for-profit businesses are blurring as a pragmatic new generation of entrepreneurs, investors, and philanthropists comes onto the scene determined to use the tools of business to address the urgent need for action to combat economic injustice and environmental damage. *Mission, Inc.* surveys this landscape, drawing upon the authors' extensive personal experience managing social enterprises and on dozens of other well-chosen examples from the membership of Social Venture Network, the Social Enterprise Alliance, and other sources.

By bringing to life through stories and concrete examples the issues that confront the social entrepreneur in the United States, Lynch and Walls have crafted an eminently practical book that fully lives up to its subtitle, "The Practitioner's Guide to Social Enterprise." This volume is no academic exercise in intellectual flimflammery. It comes to grips with the often painful and protracted dilemmas facing anyone who leads a business enterprise that seeks to make the world a better place. A glance at the table of contents will prove the point.

Whether you're running a social enterprise, planning to set one up, or studying contemporary business at a university or a business school, you'll find *Mission, Inc.* to be illuminating, thought-provoking, and down-to-earth. You won't find anywhere a better introduction to the field of social enterprise.

MAL WARWICK

Preface

What brings you here?

It's a question you might want to ponder, and ponder well, before you get too far into running one of these things we call a social enterprise. If making a real difference for the planet and the species therein is inspiring, then this is the most inspirational work you could possibly get into. And if living your professional life within an endless series of paradoxes and tensions is your idea of a great challenge, then nothing is more challenging than what you're setting out to do. So before you sign on for it, spend some time with that question and see how your answers fits in with the story of your life.

As for what brought your friendly neighborhood authors, Kevin Lynch and Julius Walls, Jr., here, well, that's a bit of a story too.

We met each other a long time ago at a Social Venture Network conference and have been good friends as well as professional colleagues ever since. Since we are fellow practitioners of social enterprises who happen to run somewhat similar operations, we became, along the way, trusted confidants and counselors to each other.

What has always characterized the advice we've asked of and given to each other over the years has been its practical nature. Not "What's your theory about so and so?" but "What should I *do* about *this*, *now*?" When we had the opportunity to write this book about social enterprise for the SVN book series, we quickly realized that all we are qualified to talk about is life in the trenches. That's where we've lived, and certainly where we've learned, and where our mutual respect has been built. It is from this perspective that we bring you *Mission, Inc.: The Practitioner's Guide to Social Enterprise.*

Through all the joys and challenges we've found in running our enterprises, we've learned perhaps the most important lesson of all. *You won't be good at social enterprise unless you're passionately in love with the very idea of it.* From this perspective, it seems only appropriate to tell you a bit about what brought each of us to the work that we now love so much.

Kevin Lynch's Story

Although the "social" part didn't come around until much later, the "enterprise" part of social enterprise was, I suppose, always in my blood. My sisters like to tell rather unflattering stories of how I talked them into becoming my subcontractors on my paper routes at a significantly lower rate of pay than I was earning—my first encounter with the concept of profit margin.

In college, my buddy and I started a business delivering birthday cakes to on-campus students from their parents, which evolved into a related line of Finals Week Survival Kits. We talked a local banker into a $350 start-up loan. I will never forget the rush I felt about a week after sending out our first direct-mail solicitation to a few hundred parents, when we opened our post office box and found dozens of orders, checks enclosed, falling out. We paid off our loan a month later, and for the remaining three years of college I had all the pocket money I ever needed. (Most of it I spent on beer and pot, which becomes relevant to the story almost two decades later.)

I got out of college in 1980 and found a job right away at a big ad agency. The agency business was a *good* place for someone with a level of creativity, business sense, and salesmanship. But it was a *perfect* place for someone like me, who was also deceitful, manipulative, ruthless, and political. I rose quickly, on my own merits *and* on the backs of others. I was given the opportunity to work on a diverse portfolio of clients, giving me exposure to dozens of different companies, industries, and ways of doing business. I was and still am a student of how business works.

The ad agency business seduced this young man quite thoroughly. I thought it was all about sex, drugs and rock 'n' roll. In retrospect, there was no sex and there were way too many drugs, but the music was pretty good. By 1987, I certainly hadn't figured any of this out. What I thought I *had* unearthed, though, was that I was smarter than the company I worked for, so I left to start my own agency.

I do believe that the first time I ever experienced the word "humble" was in the process of starting up an agency. I was young, completely undercapitalized, and without a clue about how to really do it. It didn't help that I had never grown out of my daily use of marijuana and alcohol that stemmed back to my college days. I struggled along, trying to get something started, relying largely on my wife's income to support our young family.

It finally got off the ground in 1989 when I teamed up with some partners and we created Lynch Jarvis Jones. We had some ideas on how to run an ad agency that brought a modicum of success and profitability. It occurred to me that the agency might fulfill my desires for fame, fortune, and ego gratification. Our partnership didn't do all that well, however, due in no small part to my growing chemical dependency, which I managed to hide from my partners while becoming increasingly domineering and isolated. The partnership blew apart after a few years, and I was left owning the bones of what had been a good, if not great, little agency.

I was struggling for a way to go forward after the loss of a large portion of the agency's intellectual capital. It struck me that we had had some pretty good luck with a few social marketing clients who had happened to hire us along the way. I thought we could get a few more. We came up with the tagline "Marketing That Matters" to describe a new focus on working for meaningful clients and projects. I must stress that my intent at that point was not to change the world at all. It was only to find a niche into which I could retreat. Nobody else was occupying this space, and it was a nice positioning.

Right about this time, my addiction bottomed out. I was terrified at the prospect of continuing to smoke pot 24/7, and I was terrified at the idea of quitting. On March 6, 1994, I fell to my knees and turned my life over to a Higher Power. Thus began a love affair with the Twelve Steps of Alcoholics Anonymous that continues to make my life rich and manageable to this day.

My agency looked very different when viewed through sober eyes each morning. Twelve Step recovery is very much a *spiritual* process. I had a spiritual reawakening, which was just fine by me. But what I hadn't counted on was that this spiritual reawakening would, of necessity, lead to a *social* reawakening. When that happened, I was suddenly in big trouble. I came to believe rather quickly that I was in a fundamentally corrupt industry. At best, I came to believe, advertising is a meaningless little device that trivializes the sacred and magnifies the mundane.[1] And at its worst, it is the fuel that feeds the consumptive frenzy that is decimating the planet, the people, and the culture.

I remember panicking when all this hit me. I had spent more than a dozen years in the ad business. I thought it was all I was cut out to do. I began to wonder if it was possible to be in the advertising business with a different purpose—not backed into a little niche of necessity but with a whole different mission that would be squarely focused on impact. And right then, quite serendipitously I was introduced to Social Venture Network. The moment I walked into my first SVN conference and met an entire community of folks who were dedicating their businesses to a social purpose, I knew I was home.

I didn't know it at the time, but I was turning Lynch Jarvis Jones into a social enterprise. Our mission was to create positive social change through the power of advertising, and we did that by doing really good work for clients, issues, and causes that were changing the world for the good. If I do say so myself, Lynch Jarvis Jones was quite a place to work. It was rewarding in more ways than I have the space to describe, including financially.

By the new millennium, though, I was getting restless. I was going to conferences and taking tours of places like Greyston Bakery that were *hands on* changing people's lives. But I was still doing what I had been doing for twenty years: getting clients, selling them ad campaigns, struggling to get the campaign produced without too much watering down, making media buys in the same old toxic media, and hoping somebody would quit flipping through the channels long enough to maybe catch the message. I started to wonder if an ad agency was really the most efficient vehicle by which to change the world.

As luck would have it, a series of events came together very quickly that gave me the opportunity to exit the agency at a financial high-water mark and get all of my stakeholders out whole as well. I jumped through the window of opportunity in 2001 and haven't looked back.

When I jumped, I hadn't a clue what I was going to do next. At the risk of turning this into the mushy book about Twelve Step spirituality that it does not intend to be, I will simply say that I turned it over to my Higher Power. I planned on taking a midlife retirement of two years. Eighteen months later, and not yet actively looking for my next gig, I learned, through a wonderful series of synchronicities, that Rebuild Resources was looking for a new president. Years earlier I had toured Rebuild. I remembered that it was a social enterprise that was helping addicts and alcoholics *just like me* get back on their feet by giving them jobs in businesses it was running. The moment I heard about the job, as I sat there with a cup of coffee, I said to myself, out loud, "I guess this is what I'm going to be doing next."

That was almost six years ago, and I'm still at Rebuild as of this writing. I can say without hesitation that this is the most difficult and the most joyful work I have ever done—by a huge margin. On my third or fourth day on the job, the bookkeeper walked in and mentioned that I might like to know that we had $45 left and payroll was due. I suggested that we would have to use that big credit line I had been told about. She clarified that we had $45 left *on the line of credit*. That same day, a young man in our program showed me his new driver's license and thanked me for Rebuild's being there because he could drive to Nebraska for the first time in ten years to see his kids—and for the first time *ever* to see them while he was sober. The most difficult and the most joyful work I have ever done, indeed, and all in the same day.

No other work that I could be doing could require so much of me as a businessman and give back so much to me as a human. The twelfth of the Twelve Steps is about keeping our own gift of sobriety by helping others attain it. When I got sober in 1994, all I wanted was to not be sick and tired of being sick and tired any more. I got what I wanted—I haven't picked up a drug or a drink in over fourteen years—but little did I know I'd be given the opportunity to change the world. That's what brought me to and keeps me at this amazing social enterprise called Rebuild Resources.

Julius Walls, Jr.'s Story

I started in the business world working for a chocolate manufacturer in the Bedford-Stuyvesant section of Brooklyn, New York, for twelve years. The chocolate factory was only a few blocks south of where I grew up in the public housing projects. The square block on which I lived was exclusively projects. Our buildings were twenty stories high, with eight apartments per floor. At least ten buildings were on my block. Using an average of five people per apartment, eight thousand people were living there. Just north of the chocolate factory was another public housing complex.

Both of these projects were predominantly African-American. At almost any given time of any given day, you could see men and boys hanging out. The unemployment rate was high. The school dropout rate was high. So when I talk about men and boys hanging out, I am talking about substantial numbers in these two complexes. Yet, if you looked at the workers providing services or simply working in the neighborhood, they weren't African-American. There were factories in the neighborhood, but most of the employees were not African-American. There were stores in the neighborhood, but none of them were owned by African-Americans. There were employees in these stores, but very, very few were African-American and none of those were behind the cash registers.

I knew a few African-American men who were successful. My father worked as a corrections officer for thirty-three years, a working man until he retired. My uncle, Furman Walls, was an educator. My maternal grandfather was a Baptist preacher. These men had a powerful impact on my life. But what is missing from this list of men is a businessman, a business leader. I can't recall ever meeting an African-American business leader during my youth. I can't recall ever meeting an African-American leader who owned something—other than occasionally meeting someone who owned a house.

At the chocolate company where I started out, I asked my boss and the owners to try offering English as a Second Language classes or forming a softball team or promoting from within. I am not claiming to be the originator of these ideas, but I was an advocate. We now know the impact these and other employee-sensitive practices can have on a business when done right. But back then, my bosses simply looked at me and asked how much money they would make from them. Today we have evidence that these types of activities can influence worker productivity through worker satisfaction. But back then, they were seen as liberal nonsense by many of the most successful businesspeople. They thought a business should simply drive its people as hard as possible, take as much as possible from its customers, and put as much as possible into the owners' pockets, regardless of the impact on the community, employees, or the world. I was an impressionable young man looking up to these successful businesspeople, and I said to myself, "They must be right; look at their success. If I am to satisfy my desire to help someone, I should volunteer at my church."

Please understand that these were not heartless men. I know for a fact that the owner and the president gave away significant dollars to charity, but there was no place for that type of thinking within the business. I know they gave people a chance, but there was limited room for risk. One of those people they gave a chance to was me. There were limited opportunities for an African-American male in the management of a successful company. This company provided me that opportunity and for that I am eternally grateful. My training as a productive business leader came from within that institution. I didn't get my bachelor's degree until 2005, when I was forty-three years old and had been president of Greyston Bakery for seven years.

While my business training began at the chocolate company, my leadership and compassion training had begun when I decided I wanted to be a priest. I pursued the priesthood through high school seminary and the middle of sophomore year at college seminary. I wanted to be a priest because I felt a calling to serve my people in general and through spiritual leadership in particular. I didn't see a black priest until the fifth grade, and that priest had traveled from Uganda to visit us. He asked the class which of us would follow God's calling to serve. Right then, I decided I would. I thought that calling meant the priesthood. I now know it meant more than that vocation. It meant how I would lead my life, through the vocation of business that eventually led me to Greyston. I never did become a priest, but I have become a minister in the African Methodist Episcopal Zion Church. And between that and Greyston, I know I am doing God's work.

I am not the same individual who arrived at the Bakery some thirteen years ago. I first encountered Greyston in 1992. I had left the chocolate company to start my own chocolate business. I called on Greyston while operating that business and doing some consulting for others in marketing and sales. I ended up volunteering to bring Greyston's cookies to the White House in 1993. Over the course of three years, I had a shifting of values that led me to be psychologically available to work there. By 1995, I had joined the then $2.5 million Greyston Bakery as a consultant in the role of director of marketing and sales. Then in early 1997, I was asked to join the Bakery as director of operations. Later that year, I was appointed CEO of the Bakery. I added the position of vice president of Greyston Foundation in 2000 and eventually senior vice president in

2003. I have been fortunate in that my ascent to president and CEO has coincided with the growth of the business and its increased renown.

My work today is a combination of business, priesthood, leadership, and advocacy. I am not easily defined. Beyond my work, I am an active husband, father, son, brother, and uncle. My experiences have shaped me into someone who wants to contribute my energies, skills, and efforts toward positive, life-changing impact. My personal mission, which I carry with me every day, reads

> Live my life in integrity, daily growing in my spiritual relationship with God; reading, studying, and meditating on His word and endeavoring to do His will.

> Love, attend and be faithful to my wife, Cheryl. Love and attend to my children, Nicole, Julius and Taylor. Love and honor my Mother and Father. Love my siblings, Denise, Monica, Gerard, Todd, and William. Remember Catherine.

> Serve my people with the guidance and wisdom of God. Be sensitive to their needs, wants and desires. Help them grow in spirit and understand all that the world offers.

This is my mission in life. I will keep it in my heart. ("For as he thinketh in his heart, so is he." Prov. 23:7)

My God-given mission has informed my decision to work in the social enterprise world as opposed to the general business world. My God-given mission influences my decisions of what I will do and what I will not do.

We came here on different paths, but our paths now converge with you and every other social enterpriser who seeks to change the world for the better through business.

What brings *you* here?

KEVIN LYNCH
St. Paul, Minnesota

JULIUS WALLS, JR.
Yonkers, New York

November 2008

Acknowledgments

From Both of Us

We want to acknowledge Fred Myers and Bernie Glassman, who founded the enterprises we are now privileged to lead. There would be no Rebuild Resources and no Greyston Bakery to write about if these entrepreneurs had sat around for the last twenty-five years waiting for a book to come out. They just did it, and we're extremely grateful they did.

Nor would this book exist without the huge contributions of a team of MBA candidates from the Bainbridge Graduate Institute on Bainbridge Island, Washington—the nation's first Sustainable Business MBA program. These guys conducted all the interviews and background research for the book, gratis, just because they wanted to advance the field. They did that on top of grad school, and, get this, they are doing *that* on top of their day jobs. They are truly amazing. You should hire them or invest in them or do whatever else you can possibly do to get next to them. All we promised them in return for their work was a plug in the book, a promise we are delighted to hereby fulfill:

- Linda Glasier (class of 2009) fights the good fight at the Washington State Department of Ecology and endeavors to advance several diversity and social justice causes.
- Michael O'Brien (class of 2010) helps to advance the greening of business media at SustainableIndustries.com and is passionate about student finance for change agents.
- Paige Coleman (class of 2008) is a strategic consultant and facilitator at Kindle Partners, works to change the

landscape of community economic development, and will seek your vote for Portland mayor in 2012.

- Robert Marino (class of 2009) works to deliver Al Gore's climate change presentations, helped cocreate the Tulip Credit Union, and cochaired BGI's Diversity and Social Justice Committee.

Contact them directly via the e-mail addresses in the back of this book to dangle rewarding, world-changing job offers in front of them.

A special thanks to Gifford and Libba Pinchot for starting a place like Bainbridge that could attract this gang and for hooking us all up together. Note to readers: There's no place like Bainbridge. Make it your first stop in the quest for brilliant, passionate MBA hires.

We have deep gratitude and endless respect for the twenty-one social enterprise practitioners who gave the benefit of their experience, wisdom, and strength, to say nothing of their time and pithy words, to the betterment of these pages. Thank you one and all.

We are deeply appreciative of Social Venture Network for being the community in which we met each other and blossomed in our careers. Special thanks to Mal Warwick for conceiving the SVN book series and encouraging us to write this book.

Thank you to Steve Piersanti for starting Berrett-Koehler, where a couple of practitioners could actually scratch together a book. He's created an amazing social enterprise in his own right. Thanks to our editor, Johanna Vondeling, for her soft but unrelenting touch; to Jeevan Sivasubramaniam for mercifully shortening his e-mail handle to jsiva so that we could cooperate with his superb attention to the myriad publishing details; and to the rest of the BK team members who are genuinely interested in helping us make this book a success.

Huge thanks to the advance readers and critiquers who had a huge impact on our content, structure and presentation. Thank you, Jerr Boschee! Thank you, Kathy Schiern! Thank you, Danielle Scott! Thank you, Tom White!

Thanks to Michelle Thorla, founder of TriskeleCorporation .com, for her speedy transcription work.

From Kevin Lynch

To the love of my life, Leslie Jean Wilson: Whatever gave you the idea that you should let me spend the first eighteen months of our marriage writing a book? Thank you for encouraging me to do this and for loving me up with those salads on my writing days. Thanks to my parents, Thomas and Barbara Lynch, and to my children, Patrick and Kerry Lynch and Austen, Mason, and Alyssa Loeffler, for all your love. To Maura Lynch, my self-appointed conscience, thank you for keeping me on the straight and narrow. And a very dear thank you to Terry Mallick, my great partner in crime and my even greater brother in recovery.

Thanks to the partners to whom I wasn't very good at Lynch Jarvis Jones: John Jarvis, Jeff Jones, and Earl Wilcox. Enduring thanks to Kris Mallick Lynch for your completely unsung role in building the agency with me despite my dark side and for not taking it away when we split. And to the whole LJJ crew over the years, with extra appreciation for Bob Ballard and Tracy McCoy: We built a social enterprise when we didn't even know what the hell that was.

To Craig Neal: This all started when you introduced me to Social Venture Network and sponsored me as a member. Thank goodness I met you. Every other member of SVN, past or present, is part of who I am today, but none more so than you whom I love the most: Pam Chaloult, Deb Nelson, Mal

Warwick, Claudia Viek, Cynthia Scharf, Doug Hammond, and my best buddy, Laury Hammel.

My gratitude goes to Rick Berglund and Tom Luukkonen for hiring me at Rebuild and hanging in there with me, to Mary Casey for working the steps with me when the going gets rough, and to every Rebuild board member who has given time, talent, and treasure to ensure our success.

To all of the Rebuild employees who work long hours for short pay: You inspire me every day with your unflinching commitment to the common good. You produce hope. Special thanks to Kevin Byker for all the back-door talks, to Lori Stee for teaching me about the three Rs, and to Josh LaBau for marketing wizardry that makes me look good.

To the nearly 1,000 courageous men and women who have put their lives back together at Rebuild: Thank you for trusting this little social enterprise to make a difference for you.

And to the late Bill W., cofounder of Alcoholics Anonymous: Thank you for envisioning a manner of living that could bring me from despair to hope in the hands of a loving and powerful God, to whom I owe all. Thank you, Higher Power, for showing me that I could and should do this with my life.

From Julius Walls

First and foremost I give honor to my God. I have not always put His will ahead of mine, but still, He has been faithful to me. My God has given me vision and provision. I owe all to Him. To God be the glory.

I thank Cheryl, my wife of twenty-four years. We have had some good times and not-so-good times. But through it all you have stood by me, supported me, lifted me, carried me, and inspired me. I love you.

I thank my children for their support and love, including coming to the office with me on their days off from school—sometimes willingly, most of the time not so willingly, but always obediently. Thank you for not beating me up when I spend long days at work or traveling around the country or work at my desk at night. I hope you do not feel you had to sacrifice too much for my work.

I thank my parents for their love and support. Through their actions they taught me the love of people. My dad also taught me about values in business before he or I understood that language. He taught me about work and taking care of family. My mother taught me about every good thing. I tell people that she gave me my taste for life.

I thank the many people at Greyston whom I have come to know and love and from whom I have learned so much: Mac McCabe, Chuck Lief, Bernie Glassman, Rodney Johnson, Lisa Saltzman, Steve Schall, Wendy Powell, Vernate Miller, David Rome, Daniel Helfman, and many, many more. Your love, support, and guidance have meant so very much to me.

And finally, I call out to a special group, the employees of Greyston Bakery. You have inspired me. I am a different person because of you. I try to do what I try to do each and every day because you get up to do what you get up to do each and every day. I have watched you overcome the challenges that life throws at you. Sometimes you do it with grace; sometimes you struggle. But you don't give up. You are teaching the world that it should not give up on you. I promise that I never will. Thank you for allowing me to be a part of your lives.

Introduction
The Most Successful Business on Earth

If you're a businessperson who has picked up this book, chances are high that you already know something pretty important: we've got to change the way things are done.

There's a big pile of problems out there: violence, poverty, environmental degradation, human rights violations, disease, and more. It's a big and daunting pile. It's so well chronicled that we needn't repeat endless statistics about its scale and scope, nor endlessly debate how things got to this point and who is to blame. The point remains: we've got to change it—and change it fast.

The good news is, things *can* change. The pleasant surprise behind this book is that business—the same institution that by any measure must bear a fair amount of the responsibility for the current situation—is also the most potent force for turning things around. In fact, hundreds of businesses are *already* hard at work doing exactly that.

The business you run, the business you're starting, or the one you're simply dreaming of can change the world for the much, much better. Make that your aim, and you'll be running the most successful business on earth.

The Power of Business

One way to understand the history of a civilization is to observe the history of its architecture. For long periods of history, the greatest power resided in the grandest seats of government and monarchy. In other epochs, the driving force of religion was located in the great cathedrals, temples, and mosques, none more magnificently than the entire city-state of the Vatican.

Today, fifty-one of the world's one hundred largest economies are corporations. The vision evoked by the very title of David Korten's seminal book, *When Corporations Rule the World*, has apparently already come true. In this age, the defining architecture of the world reflects the primacy of business, whether that be epitomized by the skyline of Manhattan, the Google campus in Palo Alto, or the emerging towers of Dubai.

Many would argue, and rightly so, that commerce in general, and capitalism as its most highly evolved manifestation, is responsible for the great advances in what is generally accepted as our improved quality of life. Whether you're a fan of sliced bread or of the greatest thing since (as of this writing, the iPhone, in the authors' humble opinion), you can chalk it all up to business.

The mantra behind every successful business is repetitively simple: find a need or want and then figure out how to fill it at a cost to the seller that is less than the buyer is willing to pay to satisfy the need. Put another way, find a pain and then offer an antidote to that pain at a price below the pain threshold.

But why would anyone go to the trouble of meeting all of these buyers' needs and wants? Our system is built on the conventional wisdom that enlightened self-interest attracts sellers to the task of meeting needs. Thus, the pursuit of profit is the catalyst for the vast improvements we have seen in the human condition.

But what happens when human needs are fully met? What is the catalyst supposed to act upon then? Remarkably, it has learned to self-regenerate through a process of creating and filling *new* needs. Jerry Mander, in *Four Arguments for the Elimination of Television*, explains how this works:

The only need that is expressed in advertising is the need of advertisers to accelerate the process of conversion of raw materials with no intrinsic value into commodities that people will buy . . . The goal of all advertising is discontent or, to put it another way, an internal scarcity of contentment. This must be continually created, even at the moment when one has finally bought something. In that event, advertising has the task of creating discontent with what has just been bought, since once that act is completed, the purchase has no further benefit to the market system. The newly purchased commodity must be gotten rid of and replaced by the "need" for a new commodity as soon as possible.[1]

Underlying the propensity of the need-inventing market system to propagate itself is a deeper driving force. That force is an insatiable hunger for continual economic growth that stems from ownership of the market system itself. Marjorie Kelly has devoted an entire amazing volume to this idea, aptly named *The Divine Right of Capital*. She argues that many different stakeholders have an interest in the course of the market system. But only one, ownership, is awarded a *preeminent* right that trumps those of the other stakeholders:

If we go rummaging through [capitalism's] entire basket of economic ideas—supply and demand, competition, profit, self-interest, wealth-creation, and so forth—we'll find most concepts are sturdy and healthy, well worth keeping. But we'll also find one concept that is inconsistent with the others . . . and it is these four words: maximizing returns to shareholders.[2]

Throughout this highly recommended work, Kelly crafts a powerful argument that the market system—the same well-intentioned organism that has broadly raised the quality of our life and civilization—creates havoc and ultimately threatens our survival by awarding "economic sovereignty" to ownership at the expense of employees, the community, and by extension, the natural world itself.

The primacy of ownership demands continued and growing returns. Business can meet this demand in only three ways: one, by inventing desire as Jerry Mander describes, despite the increasing raw material inputs and labor efficiencies required to satisfy those elevated passions; two, by focusing production on those who can afford to buy rather than those with the greatest unmet needs, creating vast and growing disparities between "haves" and "have-nots"; and three, by disregarding the real social, environmental, community, and human costs of production, or at the very least, by transferring those costs away from shareholders. In other words, by following the script of economic sovereignty for ownership, which does not require owners to pay their full share.

Business for the Common Good

But there's a catch to this, of which more and more of us are becoming aware. We're social beings. That means we have to live together. "Social," simply put, means "living or disposed to live in companionship with others or in a community, rather than in isolation . . . of or pertaining to the life, welfare, and relations of human beings in a community."[3]

Uh-oh. Being social beings creates a bit of a problem for business in modern times. Tasking the most powerful institution on earth with anything *other* than promoting the life, welfare, and relationships of human beings in a community just won't do. Will it?

We started with the premise that there are some pretty big problems that don't seem to be getting any smaller. It's probably no coincidence that the challenges we face are growing every bit as fast as the institution of business. This should come as no surprise as long as the institution views the common good as an expense item that detracts from the primary purpose of creating shareholder returns.

We have to do things differently. So, what if we put the power of business in the hands of people who think differently? What if the purpose of a business were to fulfill a *real* human, social, or community need? What if the goal were to return value to the community rather than push off expenses on it? What if the obligation to employees were to elevate them rather than extract from them? What if the cost of a raw material were pegged to its replenishment, not its depletion? What if profit were not the *point* of business but the *means* by which the point of a better world were achieved?

Now *that* would be a successful business—perhaps the most successful business on earth. That would be the kind of business that could go by the name of *Mission, Inc.* And it would be the kind of business that would epitomize what we call a social enterprise.

We're far from the first people to use this moniker to describe a certain type of organization doing a certain type of work. In fact, we seem to be relative latecomers. As we were writing this chapter, we Googled "social enterprise" and came up with 15,700,000 immediate references. A lot of people have called a lot of things social enterprises. Here are some of them:

- "Social enterprises are organizations which trade in goods or services, and link that trade to a social mission."[4]

- "An organization or venture that advances its social mission through entrepreneurial, earned income strategies."[5]

- "Social enterprises are typically, but not always, related to a nonprofit's tax-exempt function, and are often developed in partnership with for-profit partners. Social enterprise is a business tool often employed by social entrepreneurs."[6]

- "A business trading for a social purpose."[7]

- "A revenue generating venture founded to create economic opportunities for very low income individuals, while simultaneously operating with reference to the financial bottom-line."[8]

- "The myriad of entrepreneurial or 'self-financing' methods used by nonprofit organizations to generate some of their own income in support of their mission."[9]

- "A nonprofit venture that combines the passion of a social mission with the discipline, innovation and determination commonly associated with for-profit businesses."[10]

- "Any business venture created for a social purpose— mitigating/reducing a social problem or a market failure— and to generate social value while operating with the financial discipline, innovation and determination of a private sector business."[11]

Reasonable people hold different opinions on what constitutes a social enterprise, particularly on the question of corporate form and the closely related question of use of earnings (which we tackle as a matter of strategy in chapter 3). Yet the very existence of such wide-ranging opinions suggests that social enterprise is an idea whose time has come. And among all the ideas about social enterprise are a couple of common elements: one, that a social enterprise involves some sort of business activity; and two, that it is driven by a social purpose of some sort.

Which raises another question, which you've surely guessed by now: What is a social purpose? (And who anointed Lynch and Walls to define it?)

After all, a business cannot survive without meeting a social need, real or invented. One could craft an argument, no matter how hollow, that *any* enterprise is a social one: the NFL's purpose is to provide an escape from everyday life; the fashion industry's purpose is to create and celebrate beauty; the beer industry's purpose is to help a guy take the edge off after a hard day.

So, yes, if you really want to argue about it, every business has a social purpose. But we all know better than that. Some things really matter, and some things really don't. Those things that matter are part of what we might call the common good, and everything else just isn't. We would argue that the social purpose that is the target of any social enterprise must be squarely aligned with this concept of the common good.

The common good: it's really hard to define, but you know it when you see it. The Markula Center for Applied Ethics, drawing upon the work of philosophers, ethicists, and theologians, offers as good a working definition as any:

The common good, then, consists primarily of having the social systems, institutions, and environments on which we all depend work in a manner that benefits all people . . . Because such systems, institutions, and environments have such a powerful impact on the well-being of

Social Enterprise: Our Working Definition

The short version:

A social enterprise is a business whose purpose is to change the world for the common good.

The long version:

A social enterprise is

a business	an organization whose primary activity and means of revenue is the profitable trading of products and services, whether organized under a for-profit, a nonprofit, or some other legal or tax structure,
whose purpose	whose driving force—created by charter, form, bylaws, mission statement, governance, and/or shareholder fiat—
is to change the world	is to reform current conditions, not to maximize financial returns for ownership, although owners, too, may benefit,
for the common good.	so that the social systems, institutions, and environments on which we all depend work in a manner that best benefits all people.

members of a society, it is no surprise that virtually every social problem in one way or another is linked to how well these systems and institutions are functioning.[12]

The center gives several examples of the elements of the common good:

- An accessible and affordable public health-care system
- An effective system of public safety and security
- Peace among the nations of the world
- A just legal and political system
- An unpolluted natural environment
- A flourishing economic system

Business is a vehicle of incredible power. It can be used for the good, it can be used for the bad, or as is most often the case, it can simply be used selfishly for the merely mundane. We have to change how things are done. We have to, and we *can*, harness this power for the good. The opportunity is great because the need is great.

We need *businesses whose purpose is to change the world for the common good.* In other words, we need social enterprise.

The Practitioners

The good news is that social enterprises are already accomplishing amazing social purposes. We'll tell you about some of them throughout this book. They're doing it by landscaping properties, by selling hot dogs at ball games, and by creating art. They're doing it by making toilet paper, by running restaurants, and by doing diversity counseling. They're doing it by importing herbs and by making clothes. They're doing it by building playgrounds and by making soap. And without exception, they're doing it for the common good.

We're doing it by printing T-shirts and making brownies.

Lynch is the leader of Rebuild Resources, Inc., in St. Paul, Minnesota. Rebuild's mission is to help recovering addicts and alcoholics become sober, self-sufficient, and of service to society by offering them transitional employment in its business units. The largest of these is a custom apparel and promotions business that screen-prints and embroiders every manner of logo'd apparel and promotional good.

Walls runs Greyston Bakery in Yonkers, New York. The Bakery hires men and women who have little or no credentialed work experience, many of whom have come to Greyston with backgrounds that include homelessness, incarceration, substance abuse, welfare dependence, domestic violence, and illiteracy. It bakes for the industrial and gourmet markets and is especially renowned for its brownies. Greyston pursues the dual objectives of job creation and personal development for local residents and financial support for its parent, Greyston Foundation, which, in turn, operates several intensive self-sufficiency programs in Yonkers.

You could walk into Rebuild and Greyston and miss the fact that they are social enterprises. We have receiving departments that take in raw materials, production floors that convert the materials to finished goods, and shipping departments that send out the goods to customers. We have salespeople who sell, customer service people who serve, and accountants who count. We have profit and loss statements that break out the cost of goods, labor costs, and operating costs and balance sheets full of inventory, work-in-process, receivables, and payables.

At first blush, you wouldn't know that we are running anything other than going businesses. We wouldn't want it any other way because a social enterprise, first and foremost, *is* a business. But if you looked closer, you'd see something more.

You'd see that Greyston (a for-profit subsidiary of a non-profit parent company) is hiring whoever walks in the door, teaching him or her to bake, and diverting 100 percent of its profits to the housing, health-care, and AIDS hospice projects of its parent, Greyston Foundation. You'd see that Rebuild (a nonprofit social enterprise) is hiring people that no one else will touch, investing heavily in training them, sending them to work for its competitors, and then starting over with someone else—and taking pride in the *300 percent annual turnover* this strange model creates.

We love what we do. We've both run businesses our entire lives. We're into it. And we both found that our higher callings demanded that we put our capabilities at the service of a social purpose.

Our enterprises have enjoyed some degree of success, if measured by no other than the mere fact that they are still in business after twenty-six and twenty-three years, respectively. They've made a substantial impact in the communities in which they've operated and in the lives of the innumerable human beings who have benefited from them.

They've also faced huge challenges and have spent more than their fair share of time at the precipice. These social enterprises are *not* easy to run. Just about everything a traditional business takes for granted is a challenge for a social enterprise (and an opportunity, as we'll reveal throughout the book).

Consider that 80 percent of businesses fail after five years under the best of circumstances. Now add all the challenges of running a business as a social enterprise, and you'd be a little bit proud too.

As leaders of social enterprises, we've been blessed with work that is more gratifying than anything else we could imagine doing. Achieving any degree of success has stretched every fiber of our capacity. Along the way our processes have often seemed more error than trial. What has saved us time and time again is the good fortune of being part of some great networks of people who have helped show us the way. Mostly we've learned from other practitioners, and it is in that spirit that we offer this guide to you.

Lots and lots of people are doing this right—building sustainable social enterprises that are creating the common good in big and small ways. They're doing it in a myriad of models and industries and are located near and far. Many of them have become our friends through Social Venture Network, under whose auspices we've written this book, and the Social Enterprise Alliance, on whose board we are both privileged to serve.

Much of what we're going to tell you about running a social enterprise came from a series of interviews with some of the best practitioners in the country. Here's a brief profile of each:

Rick Aubry creates and delivers integrated solutions to profound social problems at *Rubicon Programs, Inc.*, via a landscaping business and branded bakery.

Shari Berenbach runs *Calvert Foundation*, which raises investment capital through individuals and institutions and uses it to provide affordable loans to nonprofit organizations that help underserved communities.

Scott Blackwell founded and leads *Immaculate Baking Company*, which makes incredible gourmet organic cookies and is built around a mission of supporting American folk art.

Allen Bromberger practices law at *Perlman & Perlman* and is one of the top experts in the country on the formation and financing of nonprofit business models.

Jim Fruchterman is a Silicon Valley entrepreneur who founded *Benetech*, a high-tech firm that uses technology innovation and business expertise to solve unmet social needs. The firm's global endeavors have been instrumental in improving literacy, human rights, and land-mine detection.

REDF, a nonprofit organization formerly known as the Roberts Enterprise Development Fund, provides financial investments and forms alliances with a portfolio of businesses in order to employ people who would otherwise remain living in long-term poverty. *Carla Javits* leads REDF, and *Cynthia Gair* heads up REDF's field advancement activities.

Darell Hammond is the big kid at the head of *KaBOOM!*, a national nonprofit organization that envisions a great place to play within walking distance of every child in America. To date, it has over thirteen hundred play spaces under its belt.

Mike Hannigan cofounded and coleads *Give Something Back*, a business products company that sells office supplies for less and gives the profits back to the community.

Jeffrey Hollender founded and still leads $100 million *Seventh Generation*, the leading brand of green cleaners, laundry detergent, dishwashing soap, diapers, baby wipes, tampons, recycled toilet paper, tissues, and paper towels.

Kevin Jones is one of the principals of *Good Capital*, an investment firm that accelerates the flow of capital to innovative ventures and initiatives that harness the power of the market to create sustainable solutions to some of society's most challenging problems.

Scott Leonard styles the world in organic, fair-trade fashions via the company he cofounded, *Indigenous Designs.*

Chris Mann coleads *Guayaki Yerba Mate*, which uses this unique rainforest drink as the new currency fueling reforestation projects and providing income for the indigenous peoples of South America.

Kevin McDonald helps fellow addicts and alcoholics get back on their feet at *TROSA*, a comprehensive, long-term, residential substance-abuse recovery program in Durham, North Carolina, that supports itself with the largest moving company in the Triangle area and several other ventures.

Clara Miller provides impartial analysis and flexible, frequently unsecured, financing that nonprofits typically can't get from other sources through *Nonprofit Finance Fund*, which she started twenty-five years ago and still leads.

Frederick A. Miller is CEO and lead client strategist of *The Kaleel Jamison Consulting Group, Inc.*, an internationally recognized team of facilitators and consultants with an emphasis on change, difference, and inclusion in the workplace.

Joan Pikas helps women advance from poverty by making a delightful line of gift soaps at *The Enterprising Kitchen*, which she founded in Chicago.

Mal Warwick founded and still leads *Mal Warwick Associates*, which helps nonprofits and political organizations build long-term, mutually rewarding relationships with individual donors through integrated fund-raising and marketing programs.

Judy Wicks lures people into becoming social activists feeding them well at an amazing organic, fair-trade, local focused, and community-involved restaurant called the *White Dog Cafe*, in Philadelphia.

Alfred Wise provides strategic advice to social enterprises of every stripe through *Community Wealth Ventures*, the consulting arm of *Share Our Strength*.

Lee Zimmerman and his partners started *Evergreen Lodge*, a historic hotel nestled in the woods bordering Yosemite National Park, to provide supportive employment to help young people build momentum in their lives and realize their fullest potential.

It's really their wisdom, more than ours, that we want to impart to you.

You may have noticed that 100 percent of the colleagues we have featured in this book are American practitioners—and you may wonder, as one good and honest friend did, if ours is a typically insular American perspective. Well, yes, frankly, it is an American perspective. Social enterprise is an idea that is rapidly blooming all over the globe, yet the demands of our own enterprises keep the two of us pretty close to home. As to typically insular, you be the judge. We suspect that—at the practitioner level, at least—many but certainly not all of the challenges and opportunities we and our colleagues face will be familiar to our counterparts elsewhere. To the extent you find that not to be the case, we certainly welcome your feedback.

Let's get to work.

The ten paradoxes of
social enterprise

Just like our colleagues, we love the enterprises we're running. Hardly a day goes by that we don't see a few glimmers of hope roll off the metaphorical production lines of our enterprises. At the end of the year, we proudly tabulate these incremental glimmers into a set of metrics and a report that documents the social change we've created.

But there's a brutal truth we're not as fond of discussing. It is simply this: *we're not doing enough.*

By any measure, the problems we're trying to address are getting bigger, not smaller. All the while, the aggregation of power continues within a market system that does not recognize the common good as its ultimate master.

We've approached this book as a practitioner's guide because we want to improve the *practice* of social enterprise. We want to improve the business performance of social enterprises so that they grow, succeed, and most critically, go to scale. For only by attaining scale, by becoming large enough to change the current dynamics, can these enterprises serve their social purposes with the proper degree of impact.

Intellectual honesty can be hard to come by in this line of work. It's easy to make yourself believe that *your* enterprise is changing the world because you are personally witnessing inspiring events, daily on the front lines. It's easy to resonate with the story of the man on the beach who is throwing starfish back into the sea, knowing full well he can't save all of them, most of them, or even a small fraction of them, but declaring, as he flings yet another, "I made a difference to *that* one."

And we *are* making a difference. But for the most part, when compared to the need, we are doing so in a series of relatively small, usually local, completely fragmented, and mostly inefficient enterprises scattered across the land. Anyone who could ever find a means of doing a financial analysis of the sector as a whole would undoubtedly uncover a massive amount of duplication of the costs of simply *being* social enterprises—start-up expenses, fixed overhead, and social costs.

Our purpose is to change the world. Every economy of scale that is lost to lack of scale is a lost opportunity for social change. Every ounce of energy and resource that we spend on *being* a social enterprise is an ounce that we're not spending on *doing* social enterprise. We can hardly be considered good stewards of our consumers' trust, our employees' sweat, or our backers' funds if we fail to understand this.

Rubicon Programs, Inc., is among the largest and most successful social enterprises in the employment field. Its leader, Rick Aubry, offers a sobering perspective (with acknowledgment to his colleague Jim Schorr):

> You need to be very cognizant of the cost and benefits of starting your business . . . Until there is a really big success in social enterprise, it's going to remain a marginal force in having an effect on poverty in the United States . . . All

of us have started out saying, "How are we going to make some jobs for the guys and gals walking in our doors?" and the businesses that evolved from that are small businesses that are not scalable . . . That really is going to require thinking about what is the value created by a social enterprise and what are the markets that could be turned to create a very large business.[1]

While Aubry is speaking from the perspective of a non-profit social enterprise in the employment field, his point holds equally true for *any* social enterprise seeking to make a dent in the problems that threaten the common good.

■ PRACTITIONER'S TIP
You must get better to get bigger to do more.

We've all read the statistics about business failure rates. A fact of life for anyone starting any business, social enterprise or not, is that more businesses close their doors than survive, and even more stay small than make it big. If you just go by the odds, you're not going to make it at all, much less on a scale that will make a difference.

More recently, as the field of social enterprise has grown, a spate of articles has been written about the failure rate of social enterprises, some concluding that social enterprises have not lived up to their promise. These articles have been met, in turn, by angry rebuttals from social enterprise practitioners, consultants, and associations.

To all of which we say, "Of course social enterprises fail—because *businesses* fail." In most cases, the reasons are fairly obvious, among them:

Reasons traditional businesses fail	Reasons social enterprises fail
Lack of cash	Lack of cash
Lousy marketing	Lousy marketing
Failure to innovate	Failure to innovate
Poor customer service	Poor customer service
Inefficient operations	Inefficient operations
Lack of leadership	Lack of leadership
Unhealthy culture	Unhealthy culture
Lack of business skills	Lack of business skills

The more interesting discussion, in our view, is whether social enterprises fail with the same discipline or even with the dignity of traditional failed businesses. Indeed another whole set of unique factors can detract from social enterprises' success:

More reasons social enterprises fail
Unwarranted optimism
Failure to cut losses
Belief that mission will prevail over reality

These factors operate so powerfully that they often become almost a part of the DNA of social enterprises. The passion of purpose can blind one to the hard calculated decisions that must be made to grow a business. But these factors, all representing some degree of hubris, can be overcome. They require nothing more than leaders who, at their core, understand that social enterprises demand the same levels of business discipline as any other successful enterprise.

Social enterprises can stumble in all the same ways traditional businesses can and a few more to boot. You can take comfort in knowing that every one of these traps is avoidable. You can take even *more* comfort in realizing that an equally powerful set of factors, not generally available to traditional businesses, can propel your success exponentially. For example, your mission can create a compelling marketing proposition. You have a greater-than-average chance of attracting great talent and harnessing their passion. You have a natural point of organizational focus that can streamline your processes and your decision making. And in general, lots of different potential stakeholders will start with the default position of liking you and wanting to see you do well.

The formula for building a sustainable social enterprise is actually quite simple to articulate, if not necessarily easy to execute:

■ **THE PRACTITIONER'S FORMULA**
Do all the right things a traditional business does, avoid the social enterprise traps, and grab the points of leverage that are available only to you.

After interviewing social enterprise leaders of every stripe, and through our own experience, we realized that every moving part of a social enterprise is a virtual double-edged sword of challenge and opportunity. In the chapters that follow, we apply this simple formula to these challenge-opportunity sets, one by one. If we can help you navigate around the challenges and capitalize on the opportunities, then perhaps you can improve the odds that your social enterprise will be among the businesses that succeed.

Better yet, then perhaps you can go to scale and *really* change the world.

What's on Your Mind?

When we sat down to write this practitioner's guide, we could have started just about anywhere. As practitioners ourselves, we get up every morning and face challenges and opportunities in every aspect of our enterprises. But how to translate this myriad of daily, interrelated experiences into a coherent practitioner's guide?

We determined that we would write several chapters, each addressing a related set of challenges and opportunities. One problem, though: we had dozens of challenges and opportunities to choose from—and a lot more to say on any subject than we could reasonably fit into a chapter. Perhaps because we are practitioners ourselves, our bias is always to listen to the voices and collective wisdom of others who are doing the same wonderfully gratifying, wonderfully difficult work. We do believe that this collective wisdom can help us all do better and grow in our impact. So we decided to let practitioners help us define the chapter content. We conducted focus groups at the 2007 Social Enterprise Alliance and Social Venture Network conferences and asked practitioners just like you what was vexing them most at the time.

What we discovered was an amazing consensus about the inherent tensions faced by practitioners. We call these the Ten Paradoxes of Social Enterprise:

- The First Paradox: *Doing Good Versus Doing Well*—An overriding issue that lies at the core of everything a social enterprise attempts to do is the dynamic tension between the demands of the business and the imperative to serve the common good. The most successful ones become adept at balancing impact and profit.

- The Second Paradox: *Form Versus Function*—A profound tension is played out in the social enterprise's choice of a corporate structure. A confusing array of strategic options is available, making it all the more important to choose the right structure.

- The Third Paradox: *Planning Versus Practice*—Striking a balance between figuring out what to do and just doing it is a reality for social enterprisers at every stage. Working with discipline is key.

- The Fourth Paradox: *Debits Versus Credits*—Sooner or later, the presence or lack of money will determine the impact that any social enterprise can make on the common good. A thorough, multiperspective understanding of money and financing is necessary in order to create financial health.

- The Fifth Paradox: *Do-Gooders Versus Good Doers*—Nowhere is the idea that the right people are your most important asset more true than in a social enterprise seeking to harness people's passion in a way traditional businesses can't. It is imperative to hire the best people.

- The Sixth Paradox: *Perception Versus Reality*—Social enterprises are uniquely bestowed with the opportunity to gain strong competitive advantage by taking their marketing efforts to a new level that we refer to as marketing on higher ground.

- The Seventh Paradox: *Value Versus Waste*—A common malady of social enterprises is to become so caught up with the "sizzle" of their social missions that the daily operational blocking and tackling of their businesses suffers. Successful practitioners achieve operational success by eliminating waste and leaning the enterprise.

- The Eighth Paradox: *Metrics Versus Instinct*—Unlike traditional businesses, social enterprises measure their success in terms of social impact. The intricacies of metrics and measurement are important to learn.

- The Ninth Paradox: *Growth Versus Focus*—Many people are already in tune with the imperative to grow to scale to efficiently fulfill a social enterprise's core purpose. They are equally aware of the challenges of doing so. Expanding sensibly is key.
- The Tenth Paradox: *Sweat Equity Versus Blood Equity*— Running a social enterprise is far from easy for the leader and can exact a personal toll. Long-term sustainability requires a continual commitment to personal growth and caring for self.

Take Every Word of This with a Grain of Salt

Warning: Never give or take "expert advice" too seriously. You are running a social *enterprise*. "Enterprise" implies "entrepreneur," and entrepreneurs know that doing the next right thing often defies anything you could plan for, be taught, or logically conclude you should do.

Kevin McDonald (recipient of a 2004 Social Enterprise Alliance award) tells a delightful tale of the sheer entrepreneurial opportunism that put his TROSA—now a sizable and relatively sophisticated enterprise—on the map in its early days.

Practical tips? Survival. You know what I mean? If somebody had front money, say $5 million, they'd waste a lot of it, I'm sure, because they wouldn't think about survival. A hurricane came through and devastated our place, and we went over to help the neighbors because nobody had any electricity. Then I saw a guy who knew how to use a chain saw, from the mountains of North Carolina. So, I got a geographical phone book—it goes by streets—and I mapped where the hurricane went through. We started helping him and went into business, cutting up the trees and stuff like that. It was just on a spur of the moment. That was fourteen years ago, and now I have MBAs working for me.[2]

■ PRACTITIONER'S TIP
Survive long enough to get lucky.

Your job is to make sure that your enterprise lives to fight another day. Do this enough days in a row, with the power of your social purpose and your commitment to changing the world behind you, and your break will come.

If you take seriously the survive-to-get-lucky mantra, then you shouldn't presume for a moment that the social enterprise you are starting or running today will resemble in any way the one that is going to be creating social change five or ten years from now. Remember, you're dealing with two variables: the needs of the world you are seeking to change *and* the dynamics of the industry in which your enterprise is competing.

Rubicon is today a $16 million enterprise employing 250 people and serving over 4,000 others through its programs. This is what Rubicon became, but it's *not* what Rubicon set out to become. It was initially a drop-in center for people in Richmond, California, a gathering point for very-low-income people with severe disabilities. It had no programs and its first social enterprises were very small programs that were seen more as extensions of training than anything else. For example, a plant nursery that was started in a local supermarket in the late '70s and a couple of very small cafes started in the early and mid '80s were primarily training programs that also generated some revenue.

Rubicon has evolved into an organization that today serves low-income, homeless, and mentally disabled people in the businesses, housing, and services it provides. Approximately one-third of the people currently served have a mental health disability, so its original focus is still a part, but not the largest part, of what Rubicon does. According to Rick Aubry, "The greater steps forward were when we, in the late '80s, had a transformative way of thinking about our enterprise as not being training programs that were also secondarily businesses, but that they were fundamentally businesses that, if they were successful enough, could provide training."[3]

We're all for having a great plan. As we discuss in chapter 4, you'll get nowhere fast without one—including nowhere on attracting capital to your enterprise. An entire industry of social enterprise consultants can help you with that. But remember, even the very best plans become outdated the moment you hit Save.

■ **PRACTITIONER'S TIP**
Be prepared to operate at the rate of rapidly accelerating change that every business is faced with—squared!

Putting Yourself out of Business

Of all the folks we interviewed, we admire no one more than Jeffrey Hollender, founder and CEO of Seventh Generation. Get this: despite a principled decision not to sell to Wal-Mart, Hollender acts as an unpaid adviser to that corporation on environmental and climate-change issues. He does so knowing that his efforts make the competitive landscape for his own social enterprise more treacherous, but seeing that larger companies have much more influence on the environment than Seventh

Generation. Increasingly, his goal is as much about influencing how larger companies are run as making an impact with his own business.

Interestingly enough, he notes, Wal-Mart is probably the greatest reason that his business is more competitive than it has ever been. In large part, Wal-Mart's pressure on the supply chain to be more environmentally responsible has affected the research-and-development spending of virtually every large package-goods company in America, resulting in a tremendous flow of green products into the market. While this creates stiff competition for Seventh Generation, Hollender sees it as a good thing. It has improved the landscape of products but also eliminated one of his points of difference:

> In terms of risks, the single greatest risk we face [as a company] is the awakening of our society to global warming. It has created more change in the past year then we have seen in the past nineteen years. Our challenge is to be innovative and to change the way we operate to co-exist with the competition. This means we have to move quicker and be more innovative. When there is little competition it is easier to be differentiated. When there is a lot of competition, the whole landscape changes.[4]

Why does he do it? Because he embodies the core principle of social enterprise. His actions live up to his own words: "We are not in business to be in business. We are in business only because of our mission."[5]

In fact, Hollender inspires us to reconsider our earlier-stated credo. Perhaps the credo shouldn't be "Survive long enough to get lucky" after all. Perhaps, instead, it should be "Get lucky long enough to become unnecessary."

We have to get better all right. We have to get so good that we're no longer needed.

Doing good versus doing well

BALANCING IMPACT AND PROFIT

Is yours a business idea that creates the common good? Or a social idea that gets carried out through a business model? Late at night, at social enterprise gatherings, the bars and lounges are filled with people debating this core paradox. As Shari Berenbach of Calvert Foundation says, "Mission-versus-margin is not an abstract trade-off."[1] (For the sake of this discussion, we use "margin" as shorthand for "earned operating income" simply because "mission versus margin" rolls off the tongue better than "mission versus earned operating income.")

While the trade-off defines the decisions that need to be made, you must look at the question broadly. You don't have to settle for an either-or option. In fact, the moment you do, you cease being a social enterprise. Without your mission, your commitment to the common good, your desire to cure an ill, you are not *social*. But it is equally true that without margin, you cannot define your organization as an *enterprise*.

■ **UNLOCKING THE FIRST PARADOX**
   On balance, Mission Versus Margin is not an either-or.

You need both mission and margin to be a successful social enterprise. Naturally, these two concepts will create some tension. This tension—and there *must* be tension—will push on you, your decisions, your staff, your culture, and your customer relations. It will permeate every facet of your business. You had better give it as much thought as any other part of your business, be it your financing, marketing, or administration, or else leading a social enterprise will bring out the closet schizophrenic in you and your employees.

If you find yourself thinking it is one way or another, then you are in an unhealthy place. Using the body as an analogy, is one part of your body more important than another? Would you rather do without your hands or without your feet? Would you rather have no eyes or no ears? Would you rather have a brain or a heart? What choice would you make? How would you participate in the conversation about those choices?

The body thrives when all bodily functions work in unison, each part supporting the other. So it is with the world. So it is with a social enterprise and with mission and margin. On balance, mission and margin are absolute equals. And yet on any given day, the proportions might appear to be 70/30 one way or the other. Just as it is with the body. In a track race the feet are more important to the body than the hands, but at a backyard cookout the hands carry the day. Sometimes the mission will feed the margin, and other times the margin will feed the mission. Depending on the situation, you may need to protect the mission by defending the margin or defend the margin by protecting the mission.

Mission versus margin (and margin versus mission) is, intellectually, a macro paradox. But in the day-to-day operations of a social enterprise, it is played out in an endless series of micro paradoxes.

Guiding Principles

In order to maintain some level of sanity for yourself, your board, and your employees, you must tackle these paradoxes head-on. One way to do so is by establishing a written set of guiding principles that gets all stakeholders on the same page in defining success.

Establishing these principles before you begin to operate the business is key. Doing so in the heat of battle will lead to wasted energy going in directions that will only accidentally achieve your desired outcome. You would not go to a meeting at a bank and in front of the banker calculate for the first time how much money you need to start your business. Nor would you sit in front of your customer calculating the cost of raw materials to determine your sales price. You recognize the obvious need to be prepared in those instances. Similarly, you need to be prepared for the larger decisions that will confront you. All stakeholders need to know where the values of the business lie. They need to know where you, as the business leader, stand. They need to know what will drive you and your decisions.

■ PRACTITIONER'S TIP
Create a set of guiding principles.

Guiding principles are more descriptive than a mission statement. They describe what can be expected of you in various situations. They should be prepared in cooperation with your board and employees and be readily available to them. State them as overarching principles that do not handcuff management but do provide structure and guidance. Your strategic planning and goal setting should flow from your mission and guiding principles, which should be changed only with a great deal of deliberation.

Your guiding principles should be brief, simple, and few in number. Six should be about right. While we have prepared a longer yet incomplete list to illustrate some of the potential areas your guiding principles might cover, your mileage may vary. The key principles that are important to you will depend entirely on the industry you're in and the particular "brand" of common good you are seeking to create.

Sample elements of guiding principles

Area	Questions to ask yourself
Employees	What is your role with your employees? Are they a means to an end or an intricate part of who you are? How does that manifest itself in your business and its structure?
Community	What is your relationship to your community? Is it simply a place of business? Could you move one hundred miles away without any loss of impact or connection? Or would your community miss you because you were impacting it positively?
Environment	What will you do and not do to earn a profit? What are your profit goals? Who is rewarded when a profit is made?
Wages	How will wages be calculated? What is your commitment to moving in the direction of a living wage? What type of benefits are you committed to providing?
Governance	To whom is the organization accountable? To whom are you, the leader, accountable?
Decision making	From whom are you going to seek input, counsel, and advice? Will decisions be made by consensus or chain of command? Where will the buck stop?
Business ethics	What will be the basic business terms by which you will conduct commerce?

Area	Questions to ask yourself
Diversity	Whom will you welcome into your organization and how hard will you work to get them there?
Personal development	To what degree will the enterprise be a vehicle for personal growth? To what degree will you seek to encourage spirit at work? What about fun?
Advocacy and public policy	Which social issues is the organization passionate about? Will you seek to affect those issues with your work alone? Will you be a public voice? Will you seek to influence public policy?
Impact	How will you measure your impact and what will you call success? What are you willing to spend on measurement? How open will you be to the course corrections that measurement suggests?

Once you've done the hard work of creating your guiding principles, your life will become a lot simpler. The world with which you and your enterprise interact will know where you stand.

To maximize the benefit, communicate your principles widely, including on your web site, for all to see. You will attract the stakeholders you want to work with and will repel those you don't. Life is short! Visit the Greyston Bakery web site to see an example of a set of guiding principles that leaves no confusion about what Walls and his team are up to.

Practicalities Beyond Principles

We firmly believe that a well-thought-out model, a clear set of operating principles, a combination of deep passion and commitment, and sufficient attraction of capital will, taken altogether, allow you to have both mission and margin. But again, that is a macro concept. Out there in the trenches, where you spend most of your life as the leader of a social enterprise, you face constant individual decisions where you *do* have to give more or less weight to one or the other of these imperatives.

Joan Pikas of The Enterprising Kitchen recognizes the conundrum as it relates to pricing issues in the highly competitive soap market in which she operates. She says:

> I am thrilled that we are making soap, and I think that makes us special. But at the same time, what I care about is that we are giving people an opportunity to get some work experience and get on their feet. If I thought there was a big customer out there who would buy $50,000 worth of product, which would give us a lot of work to do, but I needed to lower the per item price, which meant that we were just barely covering our costs . . . I would say "okay we are going for this because it means we are going to have x number of women here working on this project."[2]

Now, mind you, that's not a trade-off Pikas can make every day. She may need to augment that big $50,000 customer with lots of smaller, high-margin customers. Or she may need to improve the efficiency of her operations to lower her break-even point. She may need to amass more purchasing clout to lower her raw material costs. Or she may need to accept a larger portion of her budget via public support. But it's hardly an either-or, and that's the important point.

■ **PRACTITIONER'S TIP**
Most daily decisions aren't made in perfect mission-margin balance. They will tip in one direction.

Mission Leverage

Jeffrey Hollender says his company has a variety of missions:

> On the one level [our mission] is to provide safer and healthier household products to consumers. Wrapped into that is—probably equally important—our goal to both educate people about environmental, social, and health issues as well as inspire them to believe that through their actions they can make a difference. On another level—and no less important—it is to create a working experience for the people at the company that is better and more fulfilling than they have had anywhere else and that allows them an opportunity to grow and develop as human beings. In a third area, we very much wanted to be a model for what was possible in business terms of integrating our mission with our financial objectives.[3]

It is not a coincidence that Hollender has managed to build one of the most successful social enterprises (if you consider $100 million in sales and nearly 50 percent margins successful) around not just one but at least three missions—because not only can you make money while pursuing a mission, pursuing that mission can *help* you make money.

Let's start with your employees. As we discuss in chapter 6, they'll operate with a higher level of passion if they resonate with your cause. You will have the opportunity to attract better talent because your company provides more than just a paycheck. Don't use this knowledge to underpay your employees: pay them what they deserve. Their commitment to the mission will provide you an opportunity to connect with them in ways of which other businesses can only dream. People really *do* care about their planet and their fellow humans and are just waiting for an opportunity to express this. Your mission-driven business will give them that chance.

Now on to your customers. Does it matter to them that yours is a mission-driven company? The short answer is yes. The longer answer is much more complicated, as Walls learned during his early days at the Bakery. When he arrived at Greyston, the Bakery had a reputation for delicious cakes, sloppy quality control, and spotty service. The quality of the cakes and the level of service were the customers' decision factors. Everyone at Greyston *wanted* to deliver a great cake every time, on time, but intention didn't match up with performance, and many customers were not happy. Walls needed to improve on these factors or he would lose the restaurants and delis that were buying from him. No amount of connecting Greyston's unsatisfactory performance with its challenging mission would ever convince businesses to buy. They would much rather make a donation from the profits they could earn from having someone else deliver them good cakes on time than deal with a lack of performance that would reflect poorly on them to their customers.

When Walls visited these current customers and prospective customers as the director of marketing and sales, he made a conscious decision to not tell customers about the mission. He believed Greyston's performance could not stand up to its mission and didn't want to give customers the chance to blame the poor performance on the employees. He knew it was possible to raise the company's level of performance through better management of all resources, including staff. Once that was done, he could then, with confidence, reveal to his customers the source of their cakes. Many were excited to hear that their purchases benefited those less fortunate. To others, it did not matter at all.

Mission also provides positive leverage to your operations. Being good in one area tends to make you good in others. For example, before you know it you may end up greening your facilities, which tends to reduce costs, liabilities, and regulatory problems. Or you may end up getting your staff involved in community projects, leading to new customers, better suppliers, better real estate and facility options, or political support when you most need it.

Mission leads to financial leverage. In general, banks tend to be nicer to organizations that are doing good because it makes *them* look good. In the worst-case scenario (one we sincerely hope you never face), shutting down or foreclosing on a "do-good" enterprise is the last thing a bank would ever want to do. In the best case, remember that banks lend on a combination of character, capacity, and collateral and will often give more than a passing nod to the superior character of social enterprisers.

In fact, in just about every area of your enterprise, you can create a positive trade-off between mission and margin.

■ **PRACTITIONER'S TIP**
Leverage mission and margin to gain a key competitive advantage.

Of course, there are challenges too, and we'll delve into those in more detail in the chapters that follow. But the next time someone asks whether your mission is more important than your margin, tell her that your mission and margin are equally important. Tell him that you started your business because you had a yearning to change the way the world operates, that the most effective institution impacting the world today is business, and that you are going to use that power for good. Tell her that you wouldn't have started your business if you did not have this yearning for change. Tell him that you couldn't be successful without margin and wouldn't want to be without mission. Tell her that your business can't sustain itself without profits and that the world can't sustain itself without your business.

Tell him that you run a social enterprise—where mission and margin are *not* an either-or.

Form versus function
CHOOSING THE RIGHT STRUCTURE

Social enterprise leaders consistently report that finding the best legal structure for their ventures is among their very greatest challenges.

Indeed, it is almost impossible to discuss social enterprise without getting mucked up in the distinction between nonprofit and for-profit organizations. As you may have picked up from some of the definitions we quoted in the introduction to this book, some people in this field hold that the defining feature of a social enterprise is the income-generating commercial activity that supports the social mission of a *nonprofit* organization. This view is not without some underlying logic. After all, in a market system that awards divine rights to owners, how could a business that is owned by anyone other than the community as a whole put a social purpose at its absolute forefront?

That's a very valid question, we think—one that sets the standard quite high for what constitutes a for-profit social enterprise. But in fact, some companies organized as for-profits are consistently and unquestioningly driven by their social mission *ahead of* (if not completely *instead of*) shareholder enrichment. In our view, these organizations are clearly social enterprises.

We submit that the defining feature of a social enterprise is not its form but its function. In every nuance of how a social enterprise is born, grows, and becomes sustainable, its common good purpose trumps all. Once this is understood, then the enterprise's form, most specifically, its for-profit versus nonprofit status, becomes a matter of strategy toward the accomplishment of the social mission rather than a question of mission itself.

■ UNLOCKING THE SECOND PARADOX
**If the common good is your function,
then your choice of form is merely a strategy.**

In order to understand the strategic implications of your choice of form, you should first scan the existing landscape of organizational options. We would separate the landscape into two simple groups: social enterprises and non-social enterprises (or NSEs, for short).

Social enterprises, of course, we have already defined: *businesses whose purpose is to change the world for the common good*. We can then define non-social enterprises, simply, as *everything else*. At least three kinds of organizations fall within the NSE world. While we are not particularly interested in NSEs as such, they have the same array of forms as is available to social enterprises, each with certain strategic advantages and disadvantages, as we will see.

The non-social enterprise (NSE) landscape

Form	Description
Traditional business	Engages in commerce primarily to maximize returns for ownership
Socially responsible business	Seeks to maximize returns for ownership while minimizing the harmful side effects of that pursuit
Traditional nonprofit or nongovernmental organization	Seeks to achieve the common good but without a business method of doing so

So much for the world of NSEs. It's even more important to understand the social enterprise landscape. Our friend and mentor, Mal Warwick, provides a wonderfully simple analysis that separates social enterprises into four distinct quadrants, defined by their form and their methods, but unified always by their purpose.

The social enterprise landscape
(The world according to Mal Warwick)

	Social sector	Business sector
Revenue generating	Nonprofits generating revenue through business enterprises to support their social missions 1	Businesses generating revenue to support the social mission of one or more nonprofits 2
Problem solving	Nonprofits established to address a social problem in an entrepreneurial manner 3	Businesses established to address a social problem in an entrepreneurial manner 4

Quadrants 1 and 2 correspond to the revenue-generating model. In quadrant 1, Warwick points out, are parking garages operated by nonprofit hospitals to help underwrite their budgets and a plethora of other for-profit enterprises launched by nonprofit organizations to make money, pure and simple. Quadrant 2 holds remarkable ventures such as Newman's Own, Working Assets, and Give Something Back, all of which operate profitable businesses and dedicate most or all the profits to support a range of social-sector organizations.

Warwick contrasts these revenue-generating enterprises with the enterprises in quadrants 3 and 4, which are established primarily to address one or more social problems. Quadrant 3 includes organizations such as Goodwill Industries and Rubicon Programs, both of which engage in business to provide training and jobs to people who would otherwise face barriers to employment, and environmental organizations such as the Environmental Management Institute, which operates as a business but is organized as a nonprofit. In quadrant 4 lie those enterprises established as for-profit businesses but whose natures are centered on their social missions. Warwick cites ShoreBank as a prime example of a quadrant 4 enterprise—a precedent-setting bank operated and regulated like any other but dedicated to creating "economic equity and a healthy environment."[1]

Why Form Matters

Form is a strategic decision because it creates the foundation on which the structure is built and the environment in which the structure exists. Form affects

- How and by whom you are governed
- How transparently you go about making and communicating decisions

- The level of support you can expect from your community, from government, and from allied organizations in your social purpose space, and therefore your ease of doing business
- Whether and how you are taxed
- Most profoundly, everything about your capital structure, from your access to and use of capital to how profit is redeployed—all of which determines how aggressively you can invest in the growth of your enterprise

These issues are tightly interwoven. Access to capital is exponentially more important as social enterprises prepare to go to scale. Financing a social enterprise is inextricably tied up with the choice of a legal structure and the tax implications thereof. It's a complicated discussion that is becoming more so as creative legal, finance, and accounting minds work to develop new models to bring funding to social enterprises.

To do justice to this topic, we turned to Allen Bromberger, the leading attorney in the emerging and highly specialized field of social enterprise financing. In recognition of his passion and brilliance in this field, he was recently awarded the 2008 Leadership Award by the Social Enterprise Alliance. He has a great way of turning arcane legal constructs into vivid, simple concepts you can work with. He graciously provided a primer on this topic for our readers.

Strategic Implications of Social Enterprise Forms

By Allen R. Bromberger

Because social enterprises often seek to pursue business and nonbusiness objectives within a single entity, it is hard to fit them into traditional legal forms.

If the business will be capitalized primarily by *invested capital* (capital provided with the expectation that the investor will receive a financial return), a business corporation or limited liability company (LLC) is probably a better choice than a nonprofit charity as the mother ship for the enterprise. On the other hand, if the venture will be primarily financed by *donated capital* (capital for which no financial return is expected), a nonprofit mother ship will probably be best, especially if the "investors" want or need tax deductions for their contributions. But rarely will one entity suffice for a true social enterprise. Usually a combination of entities is required.

Using Nonprofits for Social Enterprise

Nonprofit corporations cannot issue shares and cannot distribute profits to "owners" the way that business corporations or LLCs can. However, nonprofits can issue debt and pay interest to lenders. So long as the rate of interest is commercially reasonable, and the purpose of the debt is to further the charity's interests rather than those of the lender, it does not matter that the lender is motivated purely by a profit motive. A charity can even create different classes of debt, each with different economic rights based on different financial arrangements.

Another significant challenge for charities that operate businesses is Unrelated Business Income Tax, otherwise known as UBIT. UBIT is a tax on income to the charity that comes from an "unrelated" business activity. A charity's income is subject to UBIT—which means it is taxed at normal corporate tax rates—if it comes from a trade or business that is regularly carried on *and that does not contribute to the charity's mission in any important way other than through the production of income*. Certain activities, such as publishing or advertising, are treated as unrelated income by the IRS regardless of whether they are related to the charity's purposes, and revenues from those activities are therefore automatically subject to UBIT.

Using For-Profits for Social Enterprise

Using a for-profit entity as the vehicle for social enterprise offers a number of business advantages. It avoids all of the restrictions of using a charity, and it allows the organizers much greater flexibility in raising capital. In addition to debt, business corporations can issue shares and pay dividends, they can enter into profit-sharing arrangements with other businesses, and they are not subject to the "reasonable compensation" rule or UBIT. A primary disadvantage of a business corporation is the fact that contributions to the business are not tax deductible, and contributions by the business are deductible only up to 10 percent of net income.

A stickier strategic implication of the for-profit form is that of governance. The managers of a business corporation have a fiduciary obligation to run the company in the best interests of the shareholders. Because the interests of shareholders is typically interpreted to mean the shareholders' *economic* interests, most experts agree that the pursuit of financial gain for the benefit of the owners is the primary function of a business corporation. A case can be made, however, that the shareholders' interests in a social enterprise include the accomplishment of social outcomes, especially when the shareholders themselves have included a provision to that effect in a well-drafted shareholder's agreement. In such a case, the managers' duty would extend to producing social outcomes as well as profits.

Another business form that lends itself to social enterprise is the LLC. LLCs differ from corporations in that they are formed and owned by "members" rather than "shareholders" and they offer pass-through tax treatment. That means that the income and expenses of the business are reported as though the members had incurred them directly, and any profit or loss is taxed at the ownership level, rather than the entity level. Thus, if one member of the LLC is a business corporation, and another is a charity, the business corporation would pay tax on its profits, but the charity would not (assuming the business is related to the charity's purpose).

LLC laws in virtually every state allow great flexibility in structuring governance and management, much more so than the laws that govern business corporations or nonprofit corporations. LLC members have wide leeway to allocate profit and loss and management powers among themselves however they see fit, and as with business corporations, different classes of membership are permitted, each with its own economic rights.

LLCs are well-suited for enterprises with a limited number of investors and relatively low investor turnover. However, if shares are to be offered to the public or if frequent investor turnover is expected, a business corporation will probably serve better than an LLC.

Using a Joint Venture for Social Enterprise
Nonprofit corporations, business corporations, and LLCs can all participate in joint ventures. So, for example, a charity and a for-profit company can form a joint venture using an LLC as the vehicle for the enterprise and use the operating agreement to specify the rights and obligations of each member. Each member is bound by the rules that govern its own existence, so the charity may not use the joint venture to confer an undue economic benefit on the for-profit coventurer, nor may the business corporation use the joint venture to do something that it could not do directly, but in most situations, this is not a problem.

The participants in a joint venture do not, of course, have to create a separate entity as the vehicle for a joint venture. Many so-called joint ventures are created by agreement only, using such vehicles as grant agreements, financing agreements, management agreements, joint operating agreements, leases, licenses, corporate sponsorship agreements, or contracts for services.

Allen Bromberger has been an innovator in developing new and unique forms for social enterprises because he understands the conflicting advantages and disadvantages of the existing nonprofit and for-profit choices. His knack is for creating structures that offer social enterprises the best of both worlds because neither form is perfect.

Form Versus Function Trade-offs

	Nonprofit	For-profit
Governance	Accountable to the community via a board of directors	Accountable to ownership with an obligation of maximizing financial returns, unless special governance provisions are set
Transparency	Financial records available for public review via IRS Form 990	Financial records available for public review only if publicly held
External support	Some amount "built in" because of "community benefit" purpose	Earned via brand stewardship and corporate responsibility record
Taxation	None on mission-specific income; UBIT on unrelated income	All income taxable at corporate rates
Access to debt capital	Available; must be at commercially competitive rates	Available with few restrictions
Access to invested capital	Limited to donated capital, with no financial return expected	Wide access to equity investment with expectation of financial return
Use of capital	Often restricted to a donor-specified use	Generally used at the discretion of management
Use of profit	Stays within the enterprise's fund balance; may be used as internally generated capital	Available for distribution via dividends and profit-sharing in addition to use as internally generated capital

Form, Function, and Finance

Not surprisingly, several of these trade-offs have to do with the issue you'll grapple with time and again as you move your enterprise to scale: financing growth. Billions of dollars in trust funds, foundations, and endowments are issued to nonprofits for the necessary work of delivering social services in the traditional manner. This work has its place—and its limitations. Often, it has relieved symptoms of social ills, but not to the elimination of the social ills themselves. If we consider only nonprofit forms, we will be limiting our access to the investments necessary to achieve the goals desired. We will not be able to take advantage of the institution we seek to engage.

For-profit businesses have at their heart an investor, an operator, and a customer. The vast majority of investment dollars reside in the for-profit arena. We need to attract the level of investing that will allow for scale. Depending on the capital intensiveness of your industry and the capital requirements of sustainable, scalable growth, availability of capital alone may be the deciding factor on form. It certainly was for the founders of Evergreen Lodge, as Lee Zimmerman explained to us:

> We kind of let the business dictate whether we were going to go for-profit or non. It turned out to be a lot easier to show banks business plans for a real business. We also thought that it was a better model for the youth program that we wanted to do as well. The bank process is also a lot quicker than trying to get money from foundations. Banks are just faster.[2]

We predict that as more and more social enterprise leaders pursue serious scale, we will see more and more adopting the for-profit, LLC, or joint venture forms or even the new forms, such as L3C corporations or B corporations, that are emerging even as we prepare the final draft of this book.

The L3C designation, created in Vermont in 2008, allows for the creation of a hybrid between a nonprofit organization and a for-profit corporation. The entity would be a low-profit company with charitable or educational goals. The B corporation is a private designation given to organizations that pass comprehensive and transparent social and environmental screens and then institutionalize these values by amending their corporate governing documents to incorporate the interests of employees, the community, and the environment.

As unique forms of enterprise emerge, financial innovators are emerging right alongside them. At the forefront is the Good Capital organization led by our friends Kevin Jones, Tim Freundlich, and Joy Anderson. Good Cap is raising a private equity fund to invest institutionally in for-profits *and* nonprofits. Good Cap's innovation is a form of financing that acts like venture capital to the enterprise. However, unlike venture capital, it is actually structured as debt without recourse, with no claims on collateral assets. Investors are paid a contractual return if and when the enterprise hits certain benchmarks of doing well (financial performance) and doing good (mission delivery).

Jones and his colleagues are constructing a form of financing that works regardless of the nonprofit or for-profit form of the enterprise. It is crafted to meet the interests of the investor, not the constraints of the organization's form, according to Jones:

It's attractive to a particular kind of investor who doesn't just factor in risk and return. These investors factor risk and return and their impact on the world and the impact of their money in the world, so it becomes a much more philanthropically motivated investment. They apply an investment screen against realistic pro formas of future performance that we're holding these enterprises to and are expecting compliance to. And yet that's a validator of something more. They're not investing with us to make a lot of money.[3]

The moral of the story? If you want to make the greatest possible impact on the common good, you must remain open to all possible corporate forms and choose the one that fuels your enterprise's mission-delivery growth.

■ **PRACTITIONER'S TIP**
All things being equal (and they usually are not!), choose the form that finances growth.

The Final Implication of Form

Perhaps more than anything else, and more than most of us would care to admit, the choice of form affects the organizational mind-set when the hardest decisions have to be made. Jim Fruchterman, president of Benetech (which happens to be one of the strangest social enterprise forms of all, a nonprofit 501c[3] that was spun off by a for-profit Silicon Valley high-tech company and now has a wholly owned for-profit subsidiary of its own), makes a brutally honest distinction:

I get asked a lot by people, "Should I start a for-profit or a nonprofit?" And we are having a lot of debate these days about hybrid organizations. But if you divide your choices into "Am I a business with a social focus, or a nonprofit with a business method of action?" ultimately when those two bottom lines are in conflict, your organization form determines which one of those dominates. So you have to choose one or the other. And of course everyone says, "Well, we don't ever want to have to choose." Well, yeah, you don't, but there will be a day for almost every organization where you do.[4]

The very phrase "nonprofit" is actually an unfortunate accident of vocabulary that we wish would disappear altogether. It's a moniker that seems to imply that "not profitable" is an acceptable condition for a social enterprise or that "not striving to be profitable" is an acceptable strategy.

Regardless of organizational form, profit is the most undirty word in the world when it is said in the context of social enterprise. Says Clara Miller, president and CEO of the Nonprofit Finance Fund: "You don't make a business profitable by having for-profit tax status, and you can't operate a business if it is unprofitable, even if it has nonprofit tax status."[5]

■ PRACTITIONER'S TIP
Whether an enterprise is for-profit or nonprofit in form, "not profitable" is never an option.

It is true that many if not most nonprofit social enterprises have not achieved sustained profitability. That's not okay. Without profitability, they will continue to rely on public subsidy, and with public subsidy engrained in their financial models, they will never achieve the scale that we need to change the world.

Planning versus practice
WORKING WITH DISCIPLINE

We are practitioners of social enterprise. We chose to write a book focused on the practice of social enterprise because it is in the trenches of *doing* that we spend most of our time and learn the most about what really makes our enterprises tick. Not surprisingly, it's where most of the colleagues featured in this book live and breathe too. But none of us would be very good practitioners if we didn't have a healthy understanding and respect for planning.

Two seemingly contradictory quotes frame the inherent tension you will face between planning and practice. From time management guru Alan Lakein: "Failing to plan is planning to fail."[1] And from Napoleon: "No plan of battle ever survives first contact with the enemy."[2]

We believe these two views can peacefully coexist and form the basis for a healthy, sane enterprise.

■ UNLOCKING THE THIRD PARADOX
Plan well. Adjust better.

Whether you prefer to call them strategic plans or business plans, you need to have *good* plans, for many different reasons:

- A good planning process will identify your weaknesses and strengths, your opportunities and threats.

- In order to plan effectively, you will be forced to articulate the why and how of your business model. If it doesn't hold water, this will show.

- Your plans will be the basic communication documents for your engagements with banks, investors, and grantors. They will state what you will do with their money and how they will receive their return on investment.

- Your plans will guide your management team and your staff to a common understanding of what they will do together.

- Your plans will create the context for all sorts of other plans, such as your sales and marketing strategy, your staffing model, pricing, or any number of other subplans.

- Your plans will give you a means of checking your progress and staying focused on the prize: your mission and goals.

- Perhaps even more important than the plans themselves, the *process* of planning creates a forum for communication, discussion, and dialogue—at least among your internal team and potentially among other stakeholders if you choose to include them.

- And most important of all, creating and communicating and making promises about your plans will keep you, the leader, in check. And believe us, you *must* be kept in check!

Planning Well

No matter your approach to planning, business-plan writing is a specialized skill. Having the skills to operate a business does not necessarily qualify you to write a business plan. As the leader, your most important role is to articulate the vision, whether that's drawn from a process you engage in with your team or board or merely from your inspiration. However you arrive at your vision, it must be well-articulated and omnipresent in your plans.

The inherent form and structure of business plans requires those who prepare them to have complementary understandings of numbers and words. Your numbers will provide input for the critical financial analysis that is at the heart of calculating the success of your business. Your words will articulate to all stakeholders your story and vision, such that investors will provide you the capital to start and sustain your business, employees will know the direction of your business, and *you* will have the confidence to execute a well-laid-out plan.

So be realistic about your skills. If necessary, seek out someone to prepare your business plan or consider using Business Plan Pro: Social Enterprise Edition, an outstanding software platform offered by the Social Enterprise Alliance.

No matter how you get it done, make sure your plan covers the key points your stakeholders want, need, and deserve to know. As a guideline, we offer the following table of contents from the 2008 Greyston Bakery Business Plan. Walls used this plan to articulate expansion plans to his board and other current stakeholders, including staff and lenders, and as his main marketing tool to secure a non-asset-based investment.

Sample Table of Contents for Social Enterprise Business Plan
1. Executive Summary
2. Background
3. Products
4. Operations
5. Market
6. Strategy
7. Management
8. Financial Information
9. Summary

If you think this looks a lot like a business plan for *any* enterprise, you're right. What makes a social enterprise plan unique is not its structure or key points but that it is written from the perspective of an organization seeking to succeed both at commerce *and* the common good. Here's a bit more on each element of your plan.

Executive Summary

Summarize the business plan in the executive summary. This may be the only section some people read, so you have to capture their attention with a brief statement about the direction and goals of your business, how you intend to reach these goals, why you think you will be successful, and what resources you need. Write this section last. You cannot address these issues until after you complete the full planning process.

Background

Put your business into perspective. Tell the history of your organization. What is the general condition of your business and how did it get there? Speak to the financial condition to some extent, but do not get number-happy in this section. People will look for complete financial information in the financial section.

Products or Services

Describe the products or services you are selling. Distinguish between current products and services and future ones.

Operations

Describe how you intend to deliver the services or produce the products. If you offer a service, describe the service delivery model, including who will deliver the service. If you offer a product, describe the origin of the product. If you are a manufacturer, describe the manufacturing process. If you are going to purchase a finished product, describe the supply chain. Whether via a manufacturing or distributing business, describe how you intend to deliver your product to the market. Highlight any aspect of your product or service that gives you a competitive advantage. You will make reference to this again in the strategy section.

Market

The market section is big because the market is a big issue. You will need to establish two points: that people want what you have to offer and that they are willing and able to pay you what you need to be paid for it. When people complete their reading of this section, you will want them to feel confident that such a market exists.

Describe the marketplace, including opportunities and threats in the market. Who is interested in buying the product or service? Who else is selling this product or service? What is the size of the market?

Do not kid yourself into believing you do not have a competitor. That's easy to do when you have a great product and a strong mission. Walls could think his Do-Goodie (Greyston's superpremium brownie) is so good, no other brownie is a competitor. He'd be wrong. Of course, he says smugly, no brownie is as delicious as his. But he doesn't compete just with other brownies. He competes with all baked desserts. In fact, he competes with other desserts as well. As for brownies, he makes four flavors. What about the baker who makes more flavors? A customer might prefer more variety or a different texture or a lower price point or fewer calories or more. Get the picture?

Strategy

What is your competitive advantage? Prospective customers have a choice of providers. Why will they come to you? How will you let them know you exist? What is your marketing message? What is your value proposition? Why will people buy from you, and how will you articulate that? Describe your sales process. Who will be selling, and to whom will they sell? Are you using advertising and promotions? Will you have a marketing partner? Are you hiring a public relations firm to get out your message? Will you have an Internet strategy? If so, what is it?

Management

The old adage is that investors fund people, not plans. Who are the people who will execute your plan? If some key positions are open, don't be bashful in describing them. Just tell how you will fill the gaps. It is better to have an open named position than an unarticulated gap that is discovered later. You, your team, your stakeholders, and any potential investor must gain the confidence that comes from transparency.

Financial Information

Lay out your business's financial history (if it is not a start-up) and future. Both start-ups and expansions need to provide projected financial statements, including five years of profit and loss statements, current and projected balance sheets, and five years of cash flows. In addition to the annual statements, you should provide the next twelve months' profit and loss and cash flow.

If you are seeking an investment, you need to state what is formally referred to as sources and uses, defining the type of capital you seek (equity or debt, amount, and type of each) and the activities or purchases you will conduct with the money.

Summary

Provide a brief closing statement. Many business plans skip this section because the executive summary is actually the summary.

The difference between these sections is that the executive summary should be a mini–business plan, whereas the summary should be a concluding statement.

Adjusting Better

It's important to have good plans. It's equally important to not get too hung up on them. If you are going to start, grow, and scale a social enterprise capable of changing the world, you must be nimble, quick, and fast on your feet. This means you've got to be ready, willing, and able to stay ahead or move away from your best-laid plans, lest they weigh you down.

Rebuild Resources' founder developed one of the first and best models for an employment-based social enterprise designed to put some fellow alcoholics to work. But it wasn't until sometime after the plan was laid out that he actually came across the opportunity for the founding enterprise, a forklift parts and re-hab business. Thus was the business born and the enterprise christened as Rebuild Resources (for rebuilding forklifts and rebuilding lives).

A similar turn of events led to the creation of Greyston Bakery as we know it today. Early in its existence, the Bakery was mainly in the business of making pastries on a small scale to produce income for the Zen monastery that operated it. Bernie Glassman, the monastery's founder, happened to go on a social walk with a new acquaintance, Ben Cohen (of Ben & Jerry's fame), during a group meeting of what eventually became Social Venture Network. By the time the walk was over, the two of them had hatched the idea of having the Bakery make the brownies for Ben & Jerry's. The rest, as they say, is history. Today, Greyston bakes all of the brownies for inclusion in Ben & Jerry's products, including Chocolate Fudge Brownie ice cream.

Apparently, Bernie and Ben were listening to neither Alan Lakein nor Napoleon but to John Lennon, who said, "Life is just what happens to you while you're busy making other plans."[3] What happens while you're busy planning the life of your social enterprise is this:

- *Your people come or go and develop or don't*—so your capacity and expertise changes.
- *New competition emerges out of the blue or old competition folds*—so your landscape changes.
- *Old technology becomes obsolete or new technology disrupts*—so you find yourself on the leading or fading edge.
- *Funders are their fickle selves*—so your access to capital shrinks or expands.
- *Economies boom or recede*—so the psychology of customers and vendors fluctuates.
- *Commodity markets sway*—so raw material prices go up or down.
- *Success begets success and failure, failure*—so your own performance yesterday and today affects what opportunities are available to you tomorrow.

Some may argue that you can create contingency plans to mitigate the effects of "life." We think that's an arrogant argument and an unrealistic one. Your enterprise will be better served by taking a "practitioner's approach to planning."

■ **PRACTITIONER'S TIP**
Have a big vision and small plans; coordinate; inform; learn; depart, don't drift; and roll.

Have a Big Vision and Small Plans

When you're learning to drive, you go through that rough over-steering stage where you can't seem to drive straight because you are looking only a few feet ahead of the hood of the car. When the driving instructor finally tells you to look way down the road at the horizon, everything becomes smooth.

So it is with your planning. Spend your time and energy on examining, articulating, and refining the overall vision for your enterprise and reducing it to something toward which everyone can drive. For example, Rebuild's vision for the world is "that every re-entering drug addict or alcoholic becomes sober, self-sufficient and of service." KaBOOM!'s is "a great place to play within walking distance of every child in America." Benetech's is "ensuring that technology fully serves humanity."

Once you create visions of these magnitudes, your plans become less constrictive because the brilliance, creativity, and commitment of the whole organization is unleashed to head toward the horizon rather than constantly adjusting toward the plans.

Coordinate

A social enterprise has a lot of interrelated moving parts and, hopefully, a lot of empowered people. Empowered people take actions that affect, for better or for worse, what other empowered people are up to. For example, if your marketing whiz delivers more leads than your sales whiz can keep up with, or if together they deliver more orders than you have plant capacity to produce, you've got a problem—a good problem but still a problem.

If you think of a plan as a vehicle for creating an understanding of the series of interrelationships between empowered people, it will become a powerful tool for containing and focusing their collective energy.

Inform

Throughout this book we talk about the need for good, real-time information, be that your financial dashboard, your mission metrics, or your pulse on the marketplace. If you use your plan as a tool for determining what key information you need to be tracking, you will be creating a tool that can help the organization get better every single day of its life.

Learn

The smarter you get, the better your plans and your departures from them will be. Invest in institutional and industry knowledge. Go to trade shows, read industry publications, join boards, participate in blogs and Listserv groups. You must become an expert in the *actual business* you are in. In fact, given the choice between learning more about social enterprise and learning more about your industry, choose the latter. (*After* finishing this book, of course.)

Depart, Don't Drift

You will start moving away from the plan before the ink is dry. "Drifting" and "departing" are not the same. "Drifting" means doing something different than you had planned, but because not everyone knows you are doing so and those who do know don't know why, soon no one knows anything. "Departing" means making a conscious decision that the plan, as crafted, no longer fits the reality of your situation and executing an alternative. Implicit in this distinction is understanding the context of vision, coordination, and information (three of the previous points) in which that departure took place, so that the decision to depart can be properly communicated to all of the other moving parts.

Roll

If a plan doesn't live and breathe, it quickly dies. This means that it must be constantly reinvented rather than rebuilt from scratch every year or three years. When Rebuild began using the Internet as a key marketing piece, the old, simple model of developing an annual marketing plan just couldn't keep up with what was really happening out there. The planning model needed to be more dynamic, so Rebuild recently began experimenting with a rolling marketing plan model.

Lynch's marketing whiz kid came up with a different way of planning that assigns strategies and tactics to four ever-changing "buckets." He has a bunch of "foundational strategies" that look at improving the sales and marketing infrastructure. He has a set of bread-and-butter "developing strategies," the drivers that are proven to create business but need to be constantly expanded and refined. A group of "pilot strategies" contains ideas he's trying out to see if they can become drivers. And finally, the "idea bank" is a planning device, which provides a place where any idea can go to hang out until Rebuild can find the bandwidth to give it a try.

Rebuild does not yet have empirical data to show how this model will work. What is certain, though, is that the old model didn't keep up with the movement of the market. And this one does. And that is a key component of all plans!

■ PRACTITIONER'S TIP
Do the next right thing.

Your life as a practitioner is largely spent making decisions in the here and now. Given perfect data, a crystal ball, and unlimited time to ponder, you could perhaps make perfect decisions—assuming, of course, that the questions hadn't changed by the time you made them. So get real. Your goal is simply to do the best thing you can do, right now, and then do it again and again. Having a plan that examines your market, your skills and resources, and how these can work together gives you the opportunity to do just that and do it more often. Do it consistently and unwaveringly, and you'll survive long enough to get lucky.

5

Debits versus credits
CREATING FINANCIAL HEALTH

You can commit two mortal sins as the leader of a social enterprise. The first is not admitting that you know too little. The other is thinking you know it all. Nowhere are these sins more deadly than in the area of finance.

No money, no mission—it is that simple. And it is why you can't afford *not* to have a realistic understanding of money, of how it works in a social enterprise, and of your own financial literacy.

■ UNLOCKING THE FOURTH PARADOX
Continuously develop your financial literacy.

We want to arm you with practical knowledge. This chapter is not meant to turn you into a financial Wizard of Oz. It is grounded, instead, in a few key points you can use to guide your social enterprise. If you are already competent in the area of finance, we'd like to offer a few items to add to your toolbox. If finance is not currently part of your skill set, then do not let this be the last reading you do on the subject.

In this chapter, we will teach you some insider tips, provide some good financial advice, show you the gaping holes in your skill set and begin to fill them, and most importantly, inspire you to learn more.

Counting Money

We have enormous respect for Luca Pacioli, the Italian mathematician credited with inventing the double-entry bookkeeping system in Venice in 1494. It's no wonder the merchants there were of such renown. His remarkable system has stood the test of time and become the universal language for describing how money works in a business.

We speak a lot of the trade-offs and paradoxes that are part of the social enterprise world. Double-entry accounting defines those trade-offs in quantifiable, tangible terms. Its one simple rule—*that every debit creates a credit, and every credit a debit*—elegantly and perfectly portrays the financial cause and effect of every decision an enterprise makes.

■ **PRACTITIONER'S TIP**
   Debits and credits define cause and effect.

The discipline and diligence of Pacioli's system produce the two financial statements without which your enterprise cannot operate with any degree of intellectual honesty or surety. The income statement tells you *what just happened* (over any period of time you care to choose). The balance sheet tells you *where you are at right now*. Only with this understanding can you have any clue at all about *what to do next*.

It matters not whether you are running an Enron, a dot-com, or a hot dog stand, much less any of those with a primary social mission. You must understand how to count the money that flows in and out of your enterprise and how to read the statements that portray this. Uninterested as you may be in ever becoming an accountant, you must come to terms with debits and credits. You will never regret learning the fundamentals of double-entry accounting. Take a course at a community college or online or pick up a copy of *Accounting for Dummies* and you'll be well on your way.

The Money Model

Pacioli gave us a system that can describe how *any* enterprise is doing. Everything that happens in the enterprise can be described using some combination of five simple classifications:

- *Revenue*: Sources of income for the enterprise
- *Expenses*: Payments necessary to run the enterprise
- *Assets*: Items of value owned by the enterprise
- *Liabilities*: Amounts owed to outsiders
- *Equity* (termed "fund balance" in nonprofits): Amounts owed by the enterprise to its owner—in other words, what the enterprise is "worth"

These concepts may describe any enterprise, but yours is not just "any" enterprise. It's *your* enterprise, which makes it a unique organism with its own dynamics. These five classifications, and all of the subclassifications within them, can be used in endless combinations to describe what has happened, where you're at now, and what could happen in the future given various courses.

What makes your enterprise tick? Two or three key dynamics drive the financial success of any given enterprise. Rebuild happens to have three:

- The conversion rate on online leads, which drives revenue and the cost of revenue
- The placement rate for program graduates, which drives labor cost, the single highest expense item
- The markup rate on sales, which drives gross margins

And Greyston has three different ones:

- The raw material yield, which reveals the percentage of ingredients that is converted into finished products
- Pounds per labor-hour, the key measure of labor efficiency
- The market rates for cocoa, butter, flour, and sugar, which drive ingredient cost, the single highest expense item

Whatever the dynamics in your enterprise, your job is to understand them intimately, make sure everyone else in the organization does as well, monitor these dynamics constantly, and then be relentless in making them work in your favor.

■ PRACTITIONER'S TIP
Ask yourself, What are my three key dynamics?

Having Money ≠ Making Money

We entrepreneurs are an optimistic bunch. If we weren't, we wouldn't start businesses in the first place. And so when we plan, we are inclined to plan for immediate success. Most of us do not anticipate the amount of time and capital it will take to become a sustainable organization.

What do we mean by sustainable? At the end of the day, cash is king. Thus, sustainability means that more cash is coming in than going out. Better yet, it means the cash coming in covers the cost of the next sale until the next cash comes in. How much cash does that take? More than you are thinking right now. Whatever amount of cash you think it will take to succeed, multiply that by some big number and you might be close. For good measure, double *that* number just to be safe.

You must distinguish between making money and having money. When you book a sale of a product or service at a higher dollar amount than your cost, you show a profit. You've *made* money. But until you have collected the payment for that sale, you don't *have* any money other than what you had before you began the sales process. In fact, you probably have less.

Let's say you are selling salad dressing, like a certain social enterprise we all know and love. You sell the distributor $10,000 worth of salad dressing. The cost of goods sold (the ingredients, the packaging, the labor, and the shipping) for the salad dressing is $5,000. This is a pretty good deal on which you are going to make money, correct? The only issue is that the distributor promises to pay you in thirty days (and may realistically take thirty-five or forty), but you have to pay your employees next week and your suppliers in ten days. (Many suppliers will ask you to pay them up front if you are a new business.) Now you accept a second order from a different distributor for the same amount in the same month, and the cash scenario repeats itself.

In the early stages of your business, who is going to pay your bills while you wait for payment from your customers? At the outset, you may have some customers who are particularly fond of you or your mission and who may help by paying immediately or quickly. But if you do not secure additional working cash, your growth will be limited by this factor. If you did not account for the fact that you would need at least $10,000 in cash to cover the costs to make the two sales mentioned, you will be out of business.

In fact, this is a very common occurrence. Businesses with good ideas run out of cash all the time. They are under-capitalized because their leaders miscalculated either how much money they needed or how fast they were going to get it. In either case, when it came time to pay the bills, they did not have the money. The banks foreclosed, the suppliers stopped delivering, or the employees stopped coming to work because they couldn't get paid.

Learn the simple tricks of cash management.

We spent a portion of chapter 3 discussing the raising of money. But raising money is a lot more work than learning how to manage it. Five simple tricks are worth mastering. They are simple, they are straightforward, and they work.

- *Get long terms from suppliers*: Be up front with your suppliers about what you are creating. Get their support by getting their agreement to extended (forty-five-, sixty- or even seventy-five day) terms. It never hurts to ask. You'll be surprised how many say yes. As Jim Fruchterman points out, "It's nice when your vendors lend you money."[1]

- *Give short terms to customers*: Again, make this an up-front conversation with customers. Explain that your terms are ten-to-fifteen days and lean on their sympathy for your social mission if you have to.

- *Bill quickly*: Generate an invoice the moment your product leaves the shipping dock. Better yet, directly bill your customer's credit card so you get the funds the same day.

- *Make friends with your customers' Accounts Payable departments and your vendors' Accounts Receivable*: Know whom to call when you really need to get paid now or when you really need another few days to pay. Communicate constantly.

- *Minimize production cycles*: Working against your cash position is the cost you must invest in buying raw materials and paying labor before a product ever ships. Speed up the production cycle and you'll reduce the number of days between the making of these investments and the realization of a return on them.

Making Money ≠ Making Sales

Just as having money is different from making money, making money is different from making sales. Probably the biggest mistake social enterprises make, after not understanding cash, is not understanding profit.

You may have made the sale. You may have delivered the product or service, and you may even have gotten the cash in before you sent the cash out. But did you made a profit? It depends on whether you accounted for all your costs. If you sold a product, did you account for the raw materials, the waste, the labor to produce and deliver, your insurance, your rent or mortgage, your utilities, your supplies, your research and development costs, your administrative staff costs, your sales costs, and so on? If you sold a service, did you cover all of the above, less raw materials but including the labor to perform the service?

Just because you got paid does not mean you have made money. Critical to the needed understanding of finance is at least a conceptual understanding of *cost accounting*. Cost accounting is the process of allocating expenses and asset utilization to specific production units, product lines, or departments so that true profit margins can be determined.

The simple part is accounting for the *variable costs* of a sale, the actual raw material and labor inputs to the finished good, which go up or down depending on how many units you sell. Where more businesses stumble is on the apportionment of the *fixed costs*, many of which are described above, to the product units.

This is a bigger problem for social enterprises than for regular businesses. On top of all the normal fixed costs, you will have certain costs, both fixed and variable, that relate specifically to the delivery of the social mission. These tend to be softer and more difficult to calculate than typical business costs. Once identified, they are harder to allocate. If you assign them as product costs, you may price yourself out of the market. If you don't, how will they get paid? You can lower your profit target, but that will slow your growth. You can try to pay for them outside the product: in a nonprofit, by finding philanthropic support; in a for-profit, by convincing your equity holders to accept a lower return rate in consideration of your social mission.

Or, as we posit in chapter 7, you can use your social mission and the related costs to position your product at the premium-pricing end of the market, as Greyston is attempting to do with its launch of the Do-Goodie gourmet brownie.

■ **PRACTITIONER'S TIP**
Develop cost accounting practices that include the cost of the mission.

Spending Money

Even if a business can be kept going for some amount of time, being cash poor leads to bad decisions. A social enterprise cannot save its way to prosperity. At some point, it must invest real dollars into operations, real dollars into seeking out good personnel, real dollars into infrastructure, and real dollars into raw materials, or supplies. This issue will weigh on your decision making if you do not have real dollars.

Kevin McDonald started TROSA with a dream and virtually no cash. Knowing what he now knows, that's an approach he wouldn't repeat: "I'd never do it again without some front money . . . There would have to be capital up front, or whatever you guys call it, because I wouldn't do it again with $18,000 in my life."[2]

Yes, people have figured out ingenious ways to get past a lack of cash. After all, necessity is the mother of invention. And people take pride in bootstrapping their businesses. But cash-poor businesses operate with a poverty mind-set that perpetuates itself by trapping them in a cycle of continued poverty.

All businesses must spend. So in place of a poverty mind-set, we recommend a *frugal mind-set*. Let's look at how the poverty mind-set impacts personnel decisions compared to the frugal mind-set. The poverty mind-set says don't spend anything. The frugal mind-set says challenge whether you need to spend or not. The poverty mind-set says you don't need to hire; you can do it all. The frugal mind-set says don't hire beyond your needs. The poverty mind-set says hire the most inexpensive person you can find. The frugal mind-set says hire at the price you need but nothing more. If you can't beg, borrow, or steal the dollars to invest in the minimum necessary level of personnel, then you shouldn't be in business.

■ PRACTITIONER'S TIP
Have a frugal mind-set, not a poverty mind-set.

Even if you live with a poverty mind-set, you will be unable to do right by yourself, your employees, your business, and your customers. Everyone will suffer from a lack of investment into the business.

Talking About Money

By now it should be clear that you must have, at a very minimum, a good grasp of how money works. This is not to say you must be the leading expert in your organization. In fact, your management team must have complementary skill sets.

Every enterprise must have people with a sales skill set and an operations skill set. It must also have people with a finance skill set. When they started Give Something Back, Mike Hannigan and his partner brought complementary skills. Sean Marx is a sales and marketing guy, while Hannigan is more of a finance and administrative guy. Hannigan happened to be the one who could provide the financial guidance his team needed during their early stages. He understood cash flow and its impact. He understood his business's costs and how they related to pricing. He understood the importance of financial discipline and how the proper preparation of financial records would influence not only how they would do business but how they could talk with potential investors.

He also knew how to relate to banks:

> Banks would basically look at us and pull out their little bank calculator, or whatever they use, and say, "Is this a good investment of our dollars? Is this a bad investment of our dollars?" And they found that it was a good investment of their dollars. Never defaulted on a loan, we are a good, solid, well-financed company with significant net worth that has always paid its bills.
>
> So banks have not had to look at us and say, "Let's see if we have some program for the inept that we can offer you." They look it up and say, "Oh, this is a nice account. We are making money on you guys, and you are making money too." So that's a win-win for the banks, and that's important to us because that positions us in the marketplace without any assistance.[3]

Hannigan may be an extraordinary example, but let's face it: many banks, investors, and savvy funders do not have the highest regard for the financial acumen of nonprofit managers. They are suspicious of for-profit social enterprise managers as well. They don't understand how someone can have a soft heart while possessing good financial skills and the discipline to apply those skills effectively.

When you meet with the providers of capital, you must immediately dispel these thoughts with respect to yourself and your managers. The surest way to do this is to introduce them to someone in your company who knows your numbers and is in a position to do something about them.

The fact that you have a financial expert on your board who shows up once every two months will not suffice. Yes, it helps to have engaged board members who can speak intelligently about your company's mission and numbers, but the bankers and investors want to know that you have a manager looking after the assets of the company. They want to know that someone in a position of operating authority is watching the store. They want to know you have someone who understands the financial aspects of your business plan, someone who can create and monitor your cash flow. They want to know you have someone who understands the implications of loans, accounts receivable, and accounts payable.

■ **PRACTITIONER'S TIP**
The enterprise must demonstrate an institutional grasp of money.

This is not an area where you can fake expertise. Your own literacy is critical but not enough. Develop your financial bench strength as well.

Watching the Money

What systems do you need to have in place so that you can watch the store?

Shari Berenbach of Calvert Foundation gets to look at dozens of social enterprises and has concluded that a lack of basic accounting and finance systems is a substantial weakness:

> A lot of groups are very vulnerable because they have inadequate accounting systems. This is something that we focus on because we recognize that we, too, are vulnerable. Being able to track performance is really important, and many of our borrowers don't have adequate accounting and financial reporting methods. This leaves them to operate a bit in the dark. They don't know whether the social enterprise is actually generating a surplus or is draining resources.[4]

One reason for this weakness, particularly for nonprofit social enterprises, is that they typically spin out of organizations that have very different accounting systems than the kind needed for a social enterprise with moving parts. But Shari's plea for better accounting systems applies, whether you come from a for-profit or a nonprofit world.

Systems provide you and your staff the numbers you need to guide your enterprise. These numbers tell a story if you can read them. A few simple ones are absolutely indispensable to any business and universal to all (and notice that the first four are about cash):

- *Cash on hand*: What you actually have in the bank once every outstanding check clears.
- *Accounts receivable*: The amount companies or people owe you for products or services sold on credit.
- *Aging of accounts receivable*: The amount of time companies or people are taking to pay you.
- *Accounts payable*: The amount you owe companies or people for products or services sold to you on credit.

- *Aging of accounts payable*: The amount of time you are taking to pay.
- *Cash flow*: The amount of cash coming and going over some period of time, which is really nothing more than cash on hand plus accounts receivable minus accounts payable over time.
- *Revenue*: The amount you have invoiced customers (or booked as donations) over some period of time.
- *Cost of goods sold*: The expenses directly associated with producing sales, usually including raw materials, direct labor, and distribution.
- *Overhead*: All of the other expenses, including rent, leases, utilities, advertising, insurance, and administrative salaries, that can't be neatly tied to the production of revenue. (Note to self: *You are overhead!* Make it not be so. Do something every day to create revenue.)
- *Debt service*: The amount you must pay to lenders.
- *Depreciation*: The reduction in the value of your assets that occurs over time, a tricky noncash expense that essentially funds future asset purchases.

Build a system that delivers you these numbers accurately and on time and you will have the means to succeed. We recommend creating a weekly dashboard, separate and distinct from monthly or quarterly financials, that focuses solely on these key indicators.

■ PRACTITIONER'S TIP
Use a weekly dashboard of key numbers.

Reports need to be simple enough to produce timely and, more importantly, *actionable* information. While every enterprise will have a different dashboard based on its key dynamics, it's a pretty good bet that some sort of cash flow report will be a part of every one.

Cash is one of just two key indicators that serve as Walls's daily compass. He reviews Greyston's cash analysis weekly with his accountant. His short-term cash flow is a simple six-week chart based on a simple calculation that anyone can use:

■ **THE PRACTITIONER'S CASH-ON-HAND CALCULATION**
Starting cash + expected collections – expected
payments = Ending cash

He uses six weeks because this is the longest horizon for which he realistically knows his exact sales and collections. His customers place orders two to three weeks in advance and, depending on the customer, he receives payment three to six weeks thereafter. So he can fairly accurately project receipts from customers. Based on this projection, he can also estimate what he will need to pay out on the credit purchases he needs to make to complete his orders.

The other key number he looks at is his current ratio—probably the most widely used liquidity analysis. Typically a current ratio compares all current assets (cash, accounts receivable, and inventory) against all current liabilities (accounts payable and all other payments due within the coming 365 days). He uses a modification of this, eliminating inventory, because his inventory value does not fluctuate much on a weekly basis.

This is a crude method, but it never fails to point out areas of concern. The ratio should be at least 1:1, meaning he will have one dollar of cash coming in for every one dollar of cash going out. If it is not at least 1:1 but less, say 0.75:1, then at some point within the next 365 days he will not have enough cash to make his payments.

A Note on Money for Nonprofit Social Enterprises

Your world is more complicated than your for-profit counter-parts'. Clara Miller describes a dilemma you face that isn't even on the radar screen of for-profits:

> On the nonprofit side, we contend with some business-unfriendly practices—like the classic, pervasive notion that there's a standard overhead expense rate—10 to 20 per-cent—that measures efficiency, regardless of mission, size, or growth rate. Experienced managers know this is non-sense. For example, if an organization is growing fast, a good manager builds systems—say, IT personnel, equipment, and training routines—ahead of need. This increases overhead, sometimes over a few years as you catch up with the growth investment. That's good management on the for-profit side. On the nonprofit side, it's called bad management.
>
> It's illogical to focus on overhead rate as an indicator of efficiency (or of anything else, for that matter!). Those who do are mistaking an input (in the form of an imprecisely de-fined class of expenses) for an indicator of output efficiency. If your overhead leads to a cure for cancer, everyone should applaud. Managers might use overhead rate for internal managerial purposes, or government might use it in sole-source contract negotiations to develop a basis for pricing a contract without market guidance. But as a way to measure effectiveness of a charity? Or efficiency? It is simply a bad habit—and a counterproductive one.[5]

It is a bad habit, but a common one. You must become a master of the numbers that drive your enterprise—both the financials and the metrics—in order to navigate it.

Getting Good at Money

If you are going to change the world, your enterprise must rise to a level of impact. It takes money to grow. And as we have seen, it takes even more money to accomplish the common good. So anything a regular business does to become good at dealing with money, you must do doubly.

If you don't get good at gathering and then redeploying money, you'll never get a real shot at creating the common good. You create capital by understanding money, managing it, growing it, and attracting it. If you learn to do that, then you can build something quite amazing.

6

Do-gooders versus good doers
HIRING THE BEST PEOPLE

As a social enterprise, your operation faces stiff competition from the entire world of non-social enterprises: from traditional businesses in your industry, from socially responsible yet shareholder-driven businesses, and from traditional nonprofits as well.

You may also face competition from other social enterprises. Nothing would be a better indicator of social enterprise health than a marketplace in which multiple social enterprises face off in the same business markets. (Both of the authors' enterprises have at least one formidable social enterprise competitor, as is true for many others.)

But for now, most of your competition will be from NSEs. Once you absorb this premise, the lens through which you have to look at just about everything else is that of fierce competition. Of all the different ways you must compete, the one that matters by far the most is the battle for the people who are actually going to *do* your enterprise.

■ **UNLOCKING THE FIFTH PARADOX**
You can—and *must*!—win the battle for great people.

It's a formidable battle. Traditional businesses—which are masters at externalizing real costs and don't have the social costs of a common-good mission—can usually offer better wages and benefits, nicer facilities, and the appearance of more job security. Socially responsible businesses can offer all of these, along with a good feeling that the company is being a decent citizen. Traditional nonprofits can offer a sense of meaning, perhaps an appeal to nobility, an opportunity to work with kindred spirits, and in some unfortunate circumstances, even a lack of accountability that certain employees (probably not the ones you want to hire) crave.

It's a formidable battle indeed—and the one that you absolutely *must* win.

A social enterprise is a complex, demanding, constantly morphing balancing act. It requires smart people. It requires people who can look at things from more than one angle. It requires people who can live with a certain degree of uncertainty and enjoy some measure of chaos. It requires a team of people who can get through a lot.

At the simplest level of body count, your team is likely to be outnumbered. Clara Miller, whose Nonprofit Finance Fund has dramatically helped capitalize the social enterprise sector, speaks of a key distinction between the nonprofit and for-profit sectors, one that equally applies to the social enterprise and non-social enterprise sectors: "The difference between me and my counterparts on the for-profit side is that on the nonprofit side, we instinctively understaff, and on the for-profit side, they instinctively overstaff if they are going to grow. That speaks volumes."[1]

Business enterprises—social ones and otherwise—are becoming ever-more Lean (with a capital *L*, referring to the Lean Thinking movement first chronicled by James P. Womack and Daniel T. Jones in their breakthrough book by this title). Lean principles relentlessly seek out and eliminate waste in businesses, including wasted human resources. (We'll look at this phenomenon in detail in chapter 8.) You're already outnumbered, and now your competition is becoming leaner. You must become leaner yet. Better people are your best hope.

Business schools across the land are turning out legions of highly trained, highly motivated operatives—perfect weapons for market warfare. You may or may not decide you want to fight MBAs with MBAs, but you certainly can't afford to ignore or underestimate them.

Assembling the very best team available offers another advantage to a social enterprise: it is the one and only antidote to hubris, the leading occupational disease of social enterprise leaders. As a lot, we tend to be a fairly bright, confident, focused bunch. We're leading entrepreneurial ventures, operating in uncharted territory much of the time, gaining a lot of satisfaction from the change we're creating, and often getting quite an adrenaline buzz from the challenge of it all. We have a lot of the answers and the courage to improvise when we don't, all of which tends to create an environment in which others might just let us "do our thing."

■ PRACTITIONER'S TIP
Hire people who will push back!

Yes, half of our ideas are brilliant. But we rarely know which half. We can save our enterprises from ourselves only by making great hires consistently and as a matter of highest priority. Says Jeffrey Hollender,

> One of the unfortunate parts of being perceived as being successful or being wise or smart is that people think you know what you are doing. I know that is not the case

but not a lot of other people do. I try to approach each day remembering that I know very little of what there is to know and look forward to other people helping me to understand the things that I do not understand.[2]

Running a social enterprise is not for the weak of heart. In every single way we can think of, it is more complicated than running a non-social enterprise. You need better people than your NSE competitors just to play them to a draw. You need *much* better people to win.

Table Stakes

There is no substitute for good old-fashioned *dinero*.

Your mission, your working conditions, your ability to inspire and empower as a leader are all great assets. But if you truly intend to compete with traditional businesses, then your pay scales must at least be within a standard deviation or two of your competitors'. There's simply no getting around it.

Mike Hannigan's company, Give Something Back, competes with Office Depot, OfficeMax, and Staples in one of the most brutal, price-competitive industries around. He says,

> Not only do we compete for customers, but we also compete for employees. Competition for employees is based on meeting the market in compensation, benefits, and everything else. There is a twin dilemma for us. For example, the going rate for a driver is about $12 or $13 an hour for an entry-level driver. Nobody is going to get rich on $12 to $13 an hour. On the other hand, we are not going to be able to get any drivers for $10 an hour, because they are all going to go somewhere else. And if we're willing to pay $15, we are not going to be in business for very

long because our competitors who are paying $12 are obviously going to be able to exploit that cost differential by offering lower prices to the customers, who are not subsidizing a higher wage for our drivers.

The marketplace is a good measure of what is available . . . So if we want a good salesperson and that person can command $120,000 from Staples, we are going to have to pay $120,000 if we want him or her. And frankly, someone who is worth $120,000 to Staples should be worth $120,000 to us . . . We want to pay as little as we can but to get the people we need to do the job we need to do. We don't want to overpay them and we don't want to underpay them. You can't underpay them, really, because then they will go someplace else. The market takes care of that for you.[3]

Hannigan clearly understands the idea of value exchange that is at the heart of the relationship between employer and employee just as surely as between company and customer. You need to get something specific done, and getting it done has a measurable dollar value to your enterprise. The exchange needs to be reasonable.

■ **PRACTITIONER'S TIP**
Respect the value exchange at the heart of the employer-employee relationship.

If you cannot pay for the value, then you cannot expect the value to be delivered. This arrangement won't work, and it wouldn't be fair. Nor would it be a good practice for the health of the entire social enterprise sector. Darell Hammond runs KaBOOM!, one of the most meteorically successful social enterprises. He told us,

I'm pleasantly amazed and also pleased that you can't pay pauper salaries for program staff or executive staff. You have to pay for their experience and what you are asking them to do. And I think sometimes the nonprofit sector pays people so underperformingly that they move around a lot, or they are a charity themselves. They have to go to the soup kitchens on Saturdays and Sundays and be recipients of what we are trying to solve, not breaking the cycle. We have got to give them fair wages. We have to allow them to invest in the future as far as long-term compensation and retirement savings plans, and that's the only way that we are going to get ahead.[4]

The value exchange also needs to be consistent. At the leadership and management level of your social enterprise, this becomes a bit tricky as the general trends for executive compensation become more obscenely out of whack. CEOs of huge companies are making billions and of modest companies are making millions, and the escalation is not limited to the for-profit sector. While the comparative salaries for, say, production workers might be pretty consistent across any given market, the range for CEOs varies wildly from fair and reasonable to insane and incomprehensible.

A simple practice that can help make this issue a bit less sticky is simply to rely on an articulated policy. This removes executive compensation from the realm of the personal and creates an intentional, objective discussion that naturally leads to a fair, consistent, yet competitive solution, like Hannigan's:

We [the founders] knew we weren't going to be able to take any money for a year and a half. We had enough savings, and it was in our business plan that there were no salary requirements for the first year and a half, except for employees that we hired. And in our bylaws, we limit our compensation. Once we started to think about taking a salary, in the first and second years we took $2,000 a month in salary and then we took $3,000 a month and then we took $4,000 a month, depending on how the company was doing. But the bylaws limit our compensation to no more than 70 percent of what the equivalent job in an equivalent-sized company would get in this marketplace. The big accounting firms can tell you what a CEO of a $25 million office-products company makes. So we are limited to no more than 70 percent of that. But we've always been much lower than that.[5]

■ **PRACTITIONER'S TIP**
The value exchange must be fair, consistent, and competitive. But it needn't top the market.

Did you ever wonder why compensation has become so outrageous in some parts of the traditional for-profit sector? Maybe the reason is more than pure greed. Maybe it's because for-profit leaders are called upon to do things in the name of shareholder value that are so fundamentally revolting to human sensibility that you have to grossly overpay people to get them to do them. It's not enough that the leaders are overpaid, however. The worker bees must, in turn, execute the strategy and, in the same fashion, be overpaid for their complicity.

You, on the other hand, are running a social enterprise. Whatever your social mission involves, never forget that you are providing a wonderful gift to your team: the opportunity to do meaningful work. Contrary to popular belief, Hannigan points out,

Most people would prefer to make their living in a way that could provide comfort for them and their families but also enrich their lives and make them feel like they were engaged in the well-being of the life of their community. I think that's a choice that most people would make. I don't think the Donald Trump attitude is the prevailing dominant attitude.[6]

The opportunity to do meaningful work has a value on which you can literally put a dollar amount. It is the spread between the compensation level at the top of the market and the compensation you must offer to get top-of-the-market individuals to do the work of *your* social enterprise. Don't underpay, but don't overpay either.

If you find yourself in a position where you simply *can't* pay a competitive amount, then you need to rethink the underlying financial model for your enterprise. If the work that needs to be done is work that can't be fairly paid for, you have serious sustainability issues. You need to do a reality check on your entire set of operating assumptions, parameters, and projected growth rates. Revise them if necessary to focus on what you *can* do within the range of what you can afford. Do more yourself. Raise more money. Do something. But *don't* build your enterprise at the expense of your people.

You Can Find Them

At this moment in history, you have the wind at your back. All sorts of trends are expanding the pool of great people who would love to work for your enterprise. You have an exponentially growing "cultural creative" or LOHAS (lifestyles of health and sustainability) class.[7] The same folks who are creating explosive demand for organic food, green buildings, alternative energy, and hybrid automobiles want meaningful work. You have a growing disgust with corporate America, fueled by post-Enron fallout, Wall Street bailouts, oil wars, and "off-shoring." You have an entire workforce of people who came of age during wave after wave of corporate mergers and downsizings, who have no concept of working for a paternalistic corporation that can be counted on to look out for their interests.

And you have what may, by now, amount to a majority of the population who, just like you, have come to believe that we've got to change things.

These are the people who will make your enterprise soar.

Alfred Wise of Community Wealth Ventures gets the cream of the crop to work for him in his enterprise, a consulting firm that helps *other* social enterprises thrive. He says he hires "bleeding heart MBAs, people with an established business background who want to do social enterprise work . . . There is currently more talent than jobs in this kind of consulting work."[8]

■ **PRACTITIONER'S TIP**
The time is right to attract great people to social enterprise.

You'll find people of every level and with every job skill you might need. Lynch loves to talk about the blend of "beautiful people" that make up his team at Rebuild. He points out that a couple of "graybeards" like him run the finance and program areas. They bring stability, wisdom, and maturity. He has a couple of fresh, technologically savvy, energetic "young pups" doing the development and marketing. And he also has a couple of great success stories, people who have pulled themselves up from devastating circumstances through their work at Rebuild, running the production areas. It's a most unusual combination, but it works because all of these people are very, very good—and very, very committed.

Greyston makes a constant effort to keep some young blood in the building. The last several years have seen a steady stream of MBA interns, some of whom have become full-time employees. They bring energy, high spirits, and new thinking to situations. In some instances their lack of experience is an advantage because they are not limited by what has been tried and failed. You should be so lucky as to have that same "smart naiveté."

Where to find them? As good a resource as any is the landmark *Aspen Institute Guide To Socially Responsible MBA Programs*, which profiles over one hundred MBA programs with this focus. (And what a great indicator it is that over one hundred of these programs exist!) Or you can skip the guide and recruit from the best practitioner-oriented school of the bunch, Bainbridge Graduate Institute, a wonderful social enterprise in and of itself, toward which we have an admittedly deep bias and gratitude for the assistance its students provided for this book.

What a Deal You Have for Them

A social enterprise has a certain buzz about it. Notice this in one and you'll notice it in all. According to Chris Mann, you'll most certainly notice it at Guayaki: "People like to work with us due to our mission and often take a significant reduction in compensation from what they are used to. Not only are the environmental and social aspects of our business appealing, but so are the attitude and pace of business here."[9]

The attitude and pace that Mann is talking about are often experienced almost as an adrenaline rush. This feeling comes from a place of knowing that the work is important and that the social enterprise's very existence is carried on each employee's shoulders. Kevin McDonald was able to capitalize on that at TROSA: "They started coming—the people who, when you are trying to do something, understand survival, who will work sixteen hours a day, whatever it takes. And that's because of that belief in what you are doing."[10]

Mission alone isn't enough to attract and retain the kind of people you want. It needs to be backed up by well-considered practices in the everyday life of the enterprise—in other words, *how* you do *what* you do.

Four practices that are indispensable are *aspiration, say, voice, and ritual.*

Aspiration

Aspiration is your means of motivating your team with the dream of doing the impossible. You start with the deep and absolute belief that each individual absolutely *can* make a contribution to the success of the organization and, thus, to the common good. Fred Miller and his organization, The Kaleel Jamison Consulting Group hold a unique perspective on what happens in organizations that fail to understand and appreciate the importance of aspiration.

> Nobody says, "I'm going to a new job today. I want to not contribute." Nobody says, "I'm going to this new job, and guess what? I'm going to try to be the biggest screwup in the place." What people *do* say is, "I'm going to this new job. I really look forward to growing, developing, making a contribution, being valued." Then things happen inside

these organizations that make a person, who on day one was so excited and wanted to do something and wanted to make a contribution, end up feeling like "If I'm going to be treated like chopped liver, then why should I do anything? Why should I put in extra effort? Why should I think? Every time I think, they tell me to shut up. Every time I want to give them an idea, they say we don't want to hear your ideas. If that's the way they are going to treat me, that's what they are going to get." And eventually, you have a team member that you look at and say, "My God, why is that person acting that way? Why is that person just sitting in a corner? Why is that person half-doing their job?"

And I always say, When you get there, look first at the organization before you look at that person because that person didn't come in with that attitude. I can tell you, ninety-nine times out of one hundred, they didn't come in like that. Some things have happened in the organization to turn that person who had hopes and dreams and aspirations into somebody who is feeling downtrodden as a result of their experience. I know it doesn't have to be that way . . . it can be that the person comes in and makes a contribution and feels good, and their work experience helps them enhance their life experience, not only financially, but as they feed themselves as a human being on earth.[11]

Aspiration is easy to snuff out. Take care not to demotivate your staff. You hired them to do a job. Give them the tools and the resources they need and then back off. They *want* to perform. Let them.

Support aspiration by getting out of the way.

Say

The tensions and trade-offs behind every key decision in a social enterprise are complex and often intense. The more *say* you award to your staff, the better the decisions and, even more importantly, the better you'll be able to attract and retain the best and brightest to your cause.

Giving say is one of the harder things you'll do. As a leader, you'll frequently believe you already have the answers, and you know what? You won't always be wrong about that. Nor will you necessarily have a great deal of patience for the process or the time that is necessary for say to be said.

One of the best ways to create say is be intentional about creating forums for it. Rebuild created a forum called the Rebuild Council in which team members regularly sit. Any team member can create an agenda item. The council is augmented by the practice of Wisdom Circles: at any time, a team member can call a stand-up meeting of three council members to assess group conscience and make a quick decision on a pressing or timely issue. And *this* practice is backed up by weekly (and in some cases daily) meetings between the president and the council members.

Create intentional forums in which say can be said.

Voice

Whereas the idea of say is primarily an internal one, *voice* is a powerful attractant that is focused on the external. Voice is the simple practice of making your people spokespeople for your enterprise. It is a tool of enormous power. You are changing the world. The people who care most about your work are the ones doing it. Not everyone longs to be a public speaker, but you can be sure that your people consider it a privilege to talk about what you're doing.

Give them a means of doing that. Introduce them to guests. Bring them on sales calls. Let them lead tours. Send them to trade shows. Feature them in literature. Profile them on web sites. If you're clear on your mission and you communicate well internally, then there should not be a person anywhere in your organization who can't be relied on to tell your story and to tell it well—maybe even better, in fact, than you can.

■ **PRACTITIONER'S TIP**
Don't hog the fun. Give voice to all.

Ritual

This brings us to *ritual*, perhaps the most powerful and "sticky" attractant of all and one that is extremely easy to overlook. Ritual is the simple act of celebrating your social impact. Amazingly, the path of least resistance is to take the joy of the common good for granted.

Ritual makes your mission visible and cherished. At Rebuild, ritual is embodied in a weekly ceremony where clean and sober time is recognized, job placements are announced, students share their stories, and hands are held for the saying of the Serenity Prayer. At Greyston, ritual is important as well. All meetings are begun with a moment of silence to honor that the team is a confederation of individuals coming from many different places physically and mentally. The moment of silence allows people to bring themselves, fully present, to the meeting.

Chris Mann and his team at Guayaki have already identified a grand opportunity for ritual and begun planning for it: "After much work and figuring, this calculation was arrived at: a bottle a day for a year is equal to an acre of reforestation; 275,000 acres of reforestation will be equal to 100 million bottles of mate, and we only have 95 million bottles to go. That day will be a great milestone!"[12]

■ **PRACTITIONER'S TIP**
Visualize the common good through ritual.

A Fine Line

At the end of the day, you need people who can do the job. All the passion in the world does not amount to capability. Lynch learned this the hard way in the early days of his first social enterprise, a social-purpose ad agency. When he hired his first copywriter, he thought he'd found everything he was looking for: brains, commitment to the mission, understanding of social issues, and experience. There was only one problem, though: the copywriter couldn't write!

You need to have it all. You *can* have it all. The best way to get it all is to hire on talent rather than necessarily on experience. In baseball, you'd call it hiring utility infielders rather than position players.

■ **PRACTITIONER'S TIP**
Don't settle for mere talent or experience.
Go for multitool players.

Every job is different and unique to your social enterprise. A *talented* person will take a job that is reasonably matched to his or her gifts and make an extraordinary contribution. A *really talented* person will be a multitasker who can contribute in more than one place. A merely *experienced* person may do nothing more than continue a pattern of mediocrity.

Fred Miller has a knack for hiring great people, largely by having a simple conversation when he's interviewing a candidate:

> I don't care what the person has done or what credentials they have, I want to know what they have learned. And that's what I want to hear: "What have you learned in life? What have you learned about life? What have you learned about you that you could bring to this job, to this situation, to us, that will enhance us and enhance what we are trying to do and enhance you?"[13]

Get enough interesting, talented, excited people together and you'll really have something, like the team Darell Hammond has put together to drive the meteoric success of KaBOOM!. But even as you gather that team, Hammond points out, you need to also balance its skill sets and motivations very carefully:

> A lot of mission-driven organizations have a very high-intensity culture, and in high growth phases that's important, but at the same time, so is specialization. So there is always this tension between the do-gooders and the good-doers. I think it's management's job in an organization to continuously keep a fresh tension between those two, to have open and honest dialogues and discussions about your age and stage in the cycle, your priorities around hiring, and the type of people that you are hiring—to make sure that you don't compromise on the type of people so that everybody is in it for the same reason. I have made

mistakes when I have compromised on people because I thought that they would be good specialists, but they really didn't support the mission. And if they don't support the mission, people are going to ferret them out really quick, and their job is going to be really hard.[14]

It bears repeating that good people are the antidote to hubris. The ultimate measure of your capacity as a leader, according to Kevin McDonald, is your willingness to hire people who are better than you:

I've got a really good staff. My COO—he's so good. That's the thing: to find better staff than you. And it's not hard for me to find better staff than me, but what you have to do is, don't be afraid of them. Go and get them. That way you build your organization. Because it's not about you as an individual. It's about your mission. So you have to build the best staff, and that's what we are trying to do with the resources we have. I think that we have a really committed group here, and we mix it pretty good with the staff and it's great.[15]

Mediocrity has no place in an organization with the desire to change the world. Just as you must have the vision to hire the supertalented, you must have the courage to weed out and gently remove the mediocre.

Better people are all around you. Find them, get them on board, and get out of the way.

Perception versus reality
MARKETING ON HIGHER GROUND

This may just be the happiest chapter in our book.

Many of the topics we're trying to cover are tough and challenging ones, where the purpose of changing the world adds a layer of complexity and a degree of difficulty, and possibly even a measurable financial cost, to your business model. Granted, the mission usually bestows a corresponding opportunity as well.

But when you start to talk about marketing a social enterprise, you enter a realm of nearly pure opportunity to gain competitive advantage.

■ UNLOCKING THE SIXTH PARADOX
A product as good as the mission is your strongest competitive advantage.

More Than Cause Marketing

Please understand this right away, and understand it well: We are *not* talking about "cause marketing."

Cause marketing is the practice of publicly aligning a company with a high-profile cause or a nonprofit organization with which the public sympathizes. Generally, the alignment is created through the donation of promotional dollars, tied to consumer purchase of the product, to the partner organization. For example, "With each purchase of a widget between now and Christmas, we'll make a contribution to Children Without Widgets Worldwide."

Being aligned with a cause was a point of differentiation when the first cause marketers attempted it. Today, it is so widespread that its differentiating power is vastly diminished. We see distinct signs that consumers are becoming more suspicious of the sincerity and motivation of the marketer.

Entire marketing firms have devoted themselves to the practice of cause marketing. At the forefront of their new business pitches, they cite a slew of data claiming that consumers want *cause marketing*. In fact, the research says that consumers want *cause*, period. They can do without the attendant marketing.

In fact, the very litmus test of your standing as a social enterprise may be found within this discussion of cause marketing. If you are *cause*—if the reason you are here is to change things for the common good, if, as Kevin Jones of Good Capital puts it, "you'd have to dismantle the whole business in order to get rid of the mission"[1]—then you are, in our view, a social enterprise. If you are merely *marketing*—if you're just talking about a cause—you may be many things, ranging all the way from a socially responsible company to a "green-washer," but you are most definitely *not* a social enterprise.

As *cause*, you'll probably even find your enterprise approached from time to time by *marketers* who wish to make it the centerpiece of their campaigns. This is especially likely if your social enterprise uses a nonprofit form. When the offer comes, it's surely worth looking at. You could gain wonderful exposure, to say nothing of hard dollars and cents, by taking part.

But be careful. Be very, very careful. Don't talk yourself into believing that cause marketing has some purpose *other* than maximizing returns for the marketer's ownership. By definition, it can't.

Understand further that it has many pitfalls. Often, the recipient organization becomes captive to, and dependent on, the sponsoring marketer. Frequently, the core social message is co-opted by the marketer and loses its essence. Make sure your interests are fully represented at the table, not held hostage to the marketing agenda. Require a large enough, long-term enough, stable enough commitment to your organization to really make a demonstrable impact on behalf of the cause.

We also caution you to get good legal advice. Most certainly the corporations working with you have legal representation making sure the agreement document you'll sign represents their best interests. Don't do any less for your organization and cause.

And most importantly, choose your partners even more carefully than they chose you. Cause marketers are hoping that some of your fairy dust will rub off onto them. Fair enough, if the exchange of value back to your enterprise is clear and reasonable. But be keenly aware that something about the marketer will rub back onto you. It's not uncommon for a company to seek the borrowed goodwill of a good cause to counteract some bad will of its own. Be certain to do your due diligence to assure yourself that the practices and behaviors of the company are consistent with your values. Always negotiate an exit clause allowing you to disassociate from a company if it starts to deviate from your values.

■ PRACTITIONER'S TIP
Be careful about cause marketing.

Be Good

Fundraisers are fond of using the axiom "Don't give till it hurts; give till it feels good!" (Lynch has used this line himself. It works!)

But when it comes to marketing your social enterprise, you must flip the axiom on its head. Don't expect customers, even those who most keenly support your mission, to buy if it hurts. People will not accept any degree of product inferiority, or frankly even parity, just because of your social purpose.

Your mission actually sets the bar higher for your product or service. A certain sensibility among buyers demands that your offering be well above the average competitive offering. It's as though people want to be *completely* passionate about you—not just about your mission but about the mission *as it is embodied* in a superior product.

■ **PRACTITIONER'S TIP**
   Mission + mediocre product = Dissonance
   Mission + killer product = Magic

Rick Aubry put it bluntly when he told us, "The primary reason why grocery stores buy from us, or customers buy from us, is that it's the best cake in the dessert case."[2] (Those would be fighting words to Walls, were it not that Greyston sells brownies, not cakes.)

Aubry is quick to point out that mission *does* play a role. Of course it does. But it comes *after* the product, not before: "We also, of course, highlight the social good that gets achieved by a nonprofit, where the majority of the work is being done by people who otherwise would not have jobs, and 100 percent of the profits are used to fund all of the programs that we provide. In some situations, that adds value."[3]

In *some* situations, he notes, that *adds* value. But note: in *all* situations, customers want good products. More often than not, customers expect those good products to come from credible companies. In this respect, your mission might even work against you. It's not hard for consumers to figure out what you already know: that certain forces in a social enterprise business model tend to conspire against product excellence.

Rebuild Resources operates in a highly competitive business-to-business industry. Dozens of different service details, mishandled, can make a customer's life (usually that of a corporate buyer) miserable. Customers often have large-scale national logo'd apparel programs as well as smaller localized needs. Some of the very biggest customers will give Rebuild their small local orders but not the real big chunks of business. Their going-in assumption is, it's too big a risk. They question whether a company "full of junkies and drunks" can actually deliver the goods—and it's a legitimate question. They'll give Rebuild the little deals that, if they get messed up, won't really hurt them, but not the mainline business. Lynch and his team have to spend a long, long time proving themselves on the small business before the big customers will trust Rebuild with the family jewels. Once the trust develops, it's wonderful, but it's a very long process.

■ **PRACTITIONER'S TIP**
The market will assume you can't "perform" as well as a traditional business.

We have unscientifically observed that social enterprises tend to make higher-end consumer products. But many, like Rebuild, like the industrial baking division of Greyston, and certainly like Give Something Back, operate in commodity or near-commodity markets. Give Something Back, according to

Hannigan, has to actively fight the misperception that the mission bears a cost that the customer must absorb. Hannigan wants his enterprise to be held to the same standard to which a customer is holding its current vendor. But the customer often carries an unspoken objection to a presumed "hidden" social cost. Hannigan's team must fight hard to convince the customer that no sacrifice is involved in choosing his enterprise.

> We have to overcome that perception that Give Something Back is a loosey-goosey, nonprofit kind of a thing. I've gotten in trouble for saying this before, but it's kind of the Girl Scout cookie thing. We all buy Girl Scout cookies. Frankly, you could probably get these thin mints a little bit cheaper at Safeway. But we are willing to pay more to support the Girl Scouts, and we are happy to do that. But you know, businesses are not happy to do that. And they shouldn't be because they are companies. They are dependent on good economic decision making by the purchasing department to keep them competitive with the other companies in their space. So that's an objection; that's an obstacle oftentimes we have to overcome.[4]

Within the social enterprise community there is widespread admiration for KaBOOM!. Few social enterprises have grown as meteorically, and fewer yet enjoy as powerfully positive a brand identity, as Darell Hammond's organization. Yet he would argue that the success of the brand is almost entirely a matter of the product itself:

> I think that there are sometimes two types of organizations. Ones that are just really grassroots and scrappy, that do mission program work better than anybody else,

but nobody knows about them. And frankly, there are great marketing organizations that tell people that they do all this great work, but nobody actually knows what they do in the community. So the ones who say it are generally the ones who are not really doing it and the ones who are doing it, don't know how to tell people they are doing it. What we are good at is execution. We get a lot of credit for that execution, but sometimes people think we are good at marketing because of that execution of delivering a product. In fact, most of our marketing is done by our third-party partners, our sponsors that go talk us up.[5]

You had better be good—good on quality, good on service, good on value. Once you're good on those things, your mission can come shining through. That's the core of Hannigan's spaghetti sauce analogy:

I was a single guy back in the early 1990s—and single guys eat pretty much spaghetti sauce for dinner—and we had these consumer choices that we were faced with. One was Franco-American, one was Ragu, and one was Newman's Own. The three cost about the same, but one was distinguished by the fact that it had kind of an organic feel to it, less so back then, but it had a big sticker on the front that said all profits from this product are donated to national children's charities. So there I was as a consumer, wanting to spend my money wisely, spend as little as I could to get the best-tasting product, and the additional benefit was that the profits that would be in my purchasing decision would go off to support community service rather than the stockholders of Franco-American.[6]

All the mission in the world won't make someone eat a lousy, overpriced spaghetti sauce. You have to be good.

The Mission Advantage

You're making a great product, surrounding it with great service, and delivering it at a fair price. *Now* let's bring your mission to bear on your marketing.

Nobody does this better than Judy Wicks and her White Dog Cafe. Judy is fond of saying that she "uses good food to lure innocent customers into social activism."[7] Her mission *is* her marketing. It is impossible—literally impossible—to have any interaction whatsoever with Judy, with her employees, or with the White Dog itself without encountering her ubiquitous mission. Her trick? She *cocreates* the mission with her stakeholders. For example:

- She doesn't just buy from local farmers, she seeds them, she teaches her competitors how to buy from them, and she creates educational programs that teach consumers how to buy local too.
- She gives 20 percent of her profits to her foundation, solicits contributions from her customers as well, and invests the funds in customer-designated community projects.
- She hosts activist speakers at the White Dog Cafe every week.
- She takes customers on fair-trade trips.
- She publishes a newsletter with robust editorials on the issues of the day.
- She speaks tirelessly about the environment, buying local, alternative energy, and living wage all over the country.

Judy's been at it a long time, and every aspect of her mission-marketing mix is organic, down-to-earth, and personal. She has mastered the art of bringing not just the customer but all stakeholders to center stage as cocreators, or better yet, as *coconspirators*, in the accomplishment of the social purpose.

■ PRACTITIONER'S TIP
Cocreate with your customers.

Once your customer is inside your tent, no longer standing passively outside, you have a distinct advantage over your competition. Your customer is standing alongside you, satisfied by your product, committed to your mission, and willing to pay for these benefits. A customer relationship such as this can command premium pricing, attach people to customer-loyalty and frequency programs, create powerful word of mouth and buzz networks, and even, should it ever become necessary (and let's hope it never does), earn you a bit of forgiveness should you ever stub your toe.

Creating Connection

Umpteen forces are at work to commoditize and depersonalize the world. Try getting through an automated phone system to reach a real human being at your cell phone company if you need any proof. People still crave connection, perhaps even more so amidst the dearth of it. Only an enterprise authentically focused on the common good can truly deliver on that. Therein lies a tremendous advantage for you.

Here are some tricks our fellow practitioner friends are using to create connection:

- *Make the mission human*: Give it a real face whenever possible. At The Enterprising Kitchen, each soap that goes out the door is signed by the escaping-from-poverty woman who made it.

- *Connect the mission to the product's attributes*: At Rebuild, when Lynch's team is making a sales call to a large potential corporate customer, a recovering student-employee helps make the presentation. Customers love to hear what is usually an inspiring story of the employee's journey at Rebuild. But what really makes the sale is when the employee tells them "Because Rebuild has helped me turn around my life, I am going to do a great job printing your order because doing a great job for you means that we get to keep helping more and more people." The effect on the customers is profound. They don't just get to be inspired by the mission. They also get to see that they will get a better product because of it.

- *Quantify the mission whenever possible*: Find something akin to Guayakí's simple formula: "A bottle a day for a year is equal to one acre of reforestation"—to make a direct link between what you are asking a customer to do and what that action will create in the world.

- *Connect your customers not just to you but to larger movements*: Everything that KaBOOM!, its volunteers, its staff and its board do is not just about the direct connection that they are making to make kids' lives better. It's also about fertilizing and tilling the ground that makes society value kids, community, and civic responsibility in a more significant and greater way. This is what allows Darell Hammond to say, "What makes the business succeed is that it is about a movement. It's about something larger than ourselves."[8]

- *Use what you have*: When you connect customers with names and faces and movements for social change, they come to expect a lot of you. But they don't expect you to be slick and overbranded. Here's what being unslick and unpolished accomplished for Scott Blackwell at Immaculate Baking Company:

I didn't have a written business plan. I just had a basic idea of making a good product and putting it in a package that reflected the spirit of the company. So, I started with a label that featured a folk art painting, a few flavors of cookies, and not much money. Then I thought, "How do I get customers?" I figured maybe trade shows were a good solution, but then again I didn't have much cash and knew that a booth space was pretty expensive. I had noticed from walking shows that a lot of other folks had fancy pop-up displays with beautiful graphics. I ended up renting a booth space in the Atlanta market and went to work on an idea for my display. I didn't think the pop-up look really fit us anyway, so I took some old roof tin and some rough siding from an old shack and built the faux front of a house, screen door and all. The booth cost me about $27! It was awesome!

It ended up getting better: I won "Best of Show" for our display, which meant I would have a free booth space at the next show. It was a great perk, but the most important thing I learned was that I was really on to something—people loved the homemade feel of the brand. While I had hoped to write at least ten orders at the show, I ended up writing over fifty![9]

- *Bring yourself to the public in unexpected ways*: Take a page from Judy Wicks, who does not let a single opportunity for activism in greater Philadelphia go by without lending some kind of support from the White Dog; from

Rebuild Resources, which supplies printed T-shirts at cost to just about any recovery event that asks; or from Kevin McDonald, who loves to "bring the lepers out" as volunteers in his community:

> Lepers used to not leave their community; they were just isolated. And sometimes addicts can be looked at the same way. But somebody who is a mother, father, sister, brother—they are part of the community. So volunteerism from TROSA has become pretty well known in this community . . . It's socially good for the people to interact with other people and to volunteer, instead of just people volunteering to help us.[10]

- *Create ambassadors of your product or service, company, and story*: Remember what Darell Hammond claimed a few pages back. Most of the marketing for KaBOOM! is done by community partners who just can't help but talk about how much they love his organization.
- *Create multiplier effects*: A big piece of Rebuild's screenprinting business is the event T-shirt market, where a customer may order thousands of printed T-shirts for a single event. Rebuild takes the time to put a hangtag with the Rebuild story on every single piece that goes out the door. The hangtag program multiplies the impact from making one sale to one customer to reaching thousands of end users, many of whom will some day become buyers themselves for their own businesses, teams, organizations, churches or events.
- *Create opportunities for conversation*: Greyston Bakery is introducing its gourmet consumer brownie, the Do-Goodie, into retail channels with lots of in-store sampling. Certainly, Walls wants consumers to taste what is arguably the finest

brownie in the world. But equally important, he wants customers to talk with the samplers because that's how people can best learn the Greyston story.

- *Be open source*: If you're really doing social enterprise, you're doing something pretty special. People want to peek inside that and see how you do it. Let them see. Give tours. Speak publicly whenever and wherever you can. Take a page from Greyston, which publishes its open hiring model on its web site for all to see. Get real about what's proprietary (not much, when you get right down to it, in the age of Google), and share what you know. It will fascinate people. It will connect them. And hopefully it will even spawn competition, which can only make you better.

Live by Marketing, Die by Marketing

We called this the happiest chapter because, as you may have surmised, marketing is a fun and hopeful topic—so much so that you could write an entire book on it (as did our fellow Social Venture Network authors, Chip Conley and Eric Friedenwald-Fishman, in their fine volume titled *Marketing That Matters*). You should also be cautioned about a couple of items.

The first is an item of extreme sensitivity and integrity. You may be passionate, but you are not perfect, and you must never inflate what you do on the mission side any more than you should make unsubstantiated product claims. Do not allow your passion to migrate toward puffery. Be intentional about not letting your myth get ahead of your truth.

Along these same lines, even while you strive to humanize and personalize your social purpose, you must be careful to not exploit it by turning the people who benefit from your work into "poster children" for your cause. Lee Zimmerman walks this fine line every day at Evergreen Lodge:

We are talking about the youth program overtly in our marketing now, a few years into it. We have information about the program in our rooms. We announce it now in our general press releases and in our guest binders. We are starting to get news coverage that includes the way we do business with our program. [We waited awhile before we did this because] we wanted to give the program a chance to prove the model and show that we were a professional product. We didn't want to stigmatize the youth, and we didn't want to create fear for the guests or awkwardness for the youth.[11]

We advocate the simple practice of using first-person statements and testimonials from anyone you feature in your marketing. This practice honors your mission and will mean more to your public than anything a copywriter could dream up.

■ **PRACTITIONER'S TIP**
Avoid puffery that misrepresents your product or exploits your people.

You were put here to change the world. We implore you to stay true to that mission. If you do, you will gain a huge point of leverage over your competition. And your marketing efforts will be a blast. Go forth and have fun.

Value versus waste
LEANING THE ENTERPRISE

The world of business is the world of *traditional* businesses—in our parlance, the world of Non-Social Enterprises, or NSEs. Much as we'd like it to not be so, you and we recognize that social enterprises, at least at this point in the evolution of economic systems, represent but a rounding error in the sum of all the commerce that is done in the United States, much less globally.

But even when we accept for the moment that not every business is out to change the world for the common good, it's still fair to ask, Why aren't more NSEs at least modestly socially responsible? The simple answer is that most businesses think it costs too much.

■ UNLOCKING THE SEVENTH PARADOX
Eliminate waste and focus on value to achieve operational excellence and gain mission leverage.

Traditional businesses are right. The cost of the common good is real. As the traditional wisdom goes, doing the right thing squeezes your bottom line. Do you want to use environmentally safe, fairly traded, humanely produced raw materials? *Your cost of goods sold will go up.* Pay your employees a living wage, provide first-class benefits, work reasonable hours? *There goes your labor budget.* Produce in America, or closely monitor human-rights policies of offshore manufacturers? *Too expensive; say good-bye to shelf space at Wal-Mart.* Give money to the community and encourage employee volunteerism? *Less profit to reinvest in growth.* Operate from green, built-to-last facilities? *More up-front costs.*

So yes, most NSEs are inherently averse to socially responsible business practices for a "good" reason. This reason is baked right into the DNA of the underlying double-entry accounting method, which demands that every possible cost, especially the cost of doing the right thing, be externalized. Keep the environmental cost off the books by pushing it onto future generations or indigenous peoples. Keep the labor cost down by pushing it onto the families of workers. And so on. You get the picture.

It doesn't have to be this way, of course. Great minds have been hard at work devising entirely new methods of corporate reporting that give credit for internalizing the cost of social good, thereby incenting companies to do the right thing or, at least, to not do the wrong thing. This point is made by Marjorie Kelly and David Korten:

> In any socially efficient market, [wrote David Korten in *Business Ethics* magazine], "producers must bear the full cost of the products they sell," because when costs are not internalized, "a firm's profits represent not an addition to societal wealth, but an expropriation of the community's existing wealth." Externalized costs would include items like public subsidies, costs borne by injured workers, the depletion of the earth's natural capital, or the $54 billion annual cost of the health consequences of cigarettes.[1]

We take great hope in this kind of thinking. If for no other reason than its own survival, society is finally waking up to the realization that the real cost of business can't be pushed off of the corporate financial statement forever. When this is finally and inevitably understood, it will be a good day for the planet and all the peoples and species that populate it.

Even within the limitations of the existing rules for financial reporting, there is a considerable and growing realization that the cost of doing the right thing is eventually, and often very quickly, returned to the company with the foresight and vision to do so. This is why, quite independent of the social enterprise movement, more and more NSE companies even without a common good purpose, understand that *being good* is good for shareholder value. These companies have noticed that ethically produced, environmentally respectable products command better pricing, that humanely treated employees are more effective, that corporate citizenship creates more loyal customers, and that doing the right thing mitigates risk.

Enter Lean

It is against this backdrop that we now turn our attention to the subject of the actual day-to-day operations of a social enterprise and how you can (and must) aspire toward a world-class level of operational excellence. Our inspiration for this topic is the concept of Lean manufacturing, a name that is usually traced to a description of the Toyota Production System in a 1990 book by James P. Womack, Daniel T. Jones, and Daniel Roos, *The Machine That Changed the World: The Story of Lean Production*, and further developed in Womack and Jones's landmark 1996 work, *Lean Thinking*.[2]

"Lean manufacturing" is a slightly misleading phrase in that it applies equally well to nonmanufacturing environments, for example, retail and service businesses. For our purposes, we prefer to simply call the entire idea Lean. It's one of those words that works as an adjective (as in "That's a great Lean technique!"), as a verb ("Now that we're Leaning the shipping and receiving department, we need to start Leaning the office."), and as a noun ("Wow, this place could really use some Lean!").

At the heart of Lean thinking is a simple core principle:

Anything that does not add value is waste. Waste is undesirable and makes you uncompetitive and socially irresponsible. Therefore, you must relentlessly seek out and eliminate waste.

Since Womack, Jones, and Roos first popularized the notion of Lean, millions of words have been written about it, hundreds of thousands of hours of training conducted, and thousands of miles of production lines transformed. What is beautiful about it as an operating philosophy is that it is simple enough to be understood by every person in every organization and simultaneously complex enough that there is no limit to how Lean an organization can get.

To understand Lean, let's use the living example of Greyston Bakery. The core of Greyston's business is making the chocolate fudge brownies that go into Ben & Jerry's ice cream. An ice cream this amazing can only be made with amazing brownies. To make a brownie worthy of the ice cream it goes into, Greyston purchases the best all-natural ingredients, which include flour, sugar, cocoa, soybean oil, and vanilla. Greyston employees check the ingredients for quality. They meticulously measure each ingredient and in a specified manner, blend all the ingredients just so. Then they deposit a certain amount of the mixture on a tray at a certain temperature, with the same amount on each tray, and bake it at a specific temperature for a specific amount of time. They cool the baked product under controlled temperatures and then cut it to a certain size and pack it at certain temperatures.

Everything we just described makes the brownie better, which makes the ice cream better. Ben & Jerry's is happy to pay for it.

But Greyston needs to do a great deal more along the way in order to make its brownies. The cocoa, flour, sugar, soybean oil, and vanilla need to come into the plant. They need to be received, weighed, counted, and stored. They need to be moved from storage to the bakery floor. They need to be unpacked. Something needs to be done with the bags and cartons these ingredients came in. Once everything is mixed together, the mix needs to find its way to the baking pans. The baking pans need to go into the ovens. They need to come out of the ovens.

None of these activities contribute to a better brownie. Ben & Jerry's has no reason to want to pay for them. If Greyston could eliminate them altogether without hurting the product or slowing the production line—and with proper Lean attention, it *almost* could—it would get no complaint whatsoever from the customer.

Other activities happen at Greyston as well. Someone sells. Someone receives the receivables and pays the payables. The furnace filters get changed, and the bathrooms get cleaned. The payroll taxes get filed, and the health plan enrollment forms stay up to date. None of these activities make a better brownie either. But if they don't get done, no brownies can be made at all.

Through Lean eyes, Greyston's operations, like those of any enterprise, are easily classified into three groups:

- *Value-added activities*: Activities that tangibly add "form, fit, or function" for the customer. These are activities for which customers are ready and willing to pay.

- *Non-value-added activities*: Activities that add nothing to the customer's experience of the product or service. Customers have no interest in paying for such activities.
- *Non-value-added but business-essential activities*: Activities in which customers have little interest but that are necessary parts of doing business for you and your competitors.

Remember, anything that does not add value is waste, which must be eliminated. In the Greyston example, as in any Lean company, the non-value-added activities must be attacked and driven out, and the non-value-added but business-essential activities must, at the very least, be minimized.

In most of the core literature about Lean you'll find variations on a simple list of seven types of waste that were first identified in the Toyota Production System, documented by Womack, Jones, and Roos, and restated by dozens of others since then. These forms of waste and their causes are shown in the following table.

The seven kinds of waste

Type of waste	Cause
Transportation waste	Moving stuff around
Waiting-around waste	Queuing stuff up
Overproduction waste	Making too much stuff or too soon
Defect waste	Looking for bad stuff and throwing it away
Inventory waste	Letting stuff sit around
Motion waste	Moving people around
Overprocessing	Doing more to the product than the customer wants

Over a long enough period, and all other things being equal, eliminating waste is a matter of life and death. The Lean company puts more energy into value-added activities—creating better products that lead to happier customers. The Lean company puts less money into non-value-added activities—saving money that can lead to better prices, a better bottom line, growth capital, or all three. The non-Lean company gradually loses ground to the Lean rival and eventually doesn't make it.

Ultimately, the Lean company will (at least at the level of its operational approach) have the potential to be a much more responsible company than its non-Lean counterpart. True Lean disciples won't settle for conveniently externalizing waste nor the cost thereof. Lean is about eliminating it altogether. Waste is waste, no matter its form. Wasted raw materials, wasted energy costs, wasted square footage, wasted transport cost, wasted human potential, toxic leftover waste—they all have to go.

If that isn't a beautiful, socially responsible idea, we don't know what is.

■ PRACTITIONER'S TIP
Lean is one of the most socially responsible things you can do.

It's not that Lean, as widely practiced today, evolved from any advanced sense of social responsibility or anything resembling such. No, it came about simply as a means of improving quality, raising margins, reducing capital costs, and enhancing customer satisfaction—altogether, as a tool for gaining and maintaining a competitive advantage and, ultimately, for improving shareholder value. But the law of unintended consequences sometimes turns to the advantage of the common good, and this is such a case. Imagine a world where every business is completely Lean, and you'll be imagining a world where no excess costs are being dumped off the corporate financial statement onto the planet, people, and community.

Lean will contribute to *any* company's well-being. For your social enterprise, we would argue that it is even more essential. You have a high calling. At the level of the marketplace in which your enterprise operates, Lean will help you compete. And unlike your competitors, Lean or not, you cannot even consider the option of externalizing the true costs of doing business, at least if you intend to remain true to your common good commitment.

As the leader of a social enterprise, you are shooting for a different value proposition altogether. You must deliver value for your customers or else they will go somewhere else. Anything that's not adding to that value is waste, from a customer perspective, and must be eliminated. But you are simultaneously delivering value to the common good as a whole, and anything that's not creating *that* kind of value is also waste and must also be eliminated. Complicating matters further, waste of the first kind might actually be value of the second kind and vice versa.

■ **PRACTITIONER'S TIP**
For social enterprise, anything that detracts from mission is *also* waste.

You'd better be able to sort out what's waste (and what's not) and drive it from the system. You've got your work cut out for you, so you'll need some tools.

The Lean Tool Belt

The actual set of Lean tools that will help you drive both business waste and mission waste from your enterprise has yet to be invented. Your enterprise must invent them for itself because your enterprise is different from any other. Any Lean technique that is not invented inside your enterprise will not stick.

Anything that we or anyone else might offer is a set of approximations. As Rebuild's mentor in Lean thinking over the last several years has been quick to point out, Lean is a very specific philosophy that is carried out by a very generalized set of tools that each company must customize for itself. Some tools focus on increasing speed, others on reducing cost, and others on improving quality, while all of them seek out and eliminate waste.

At Rebuild, the working definition of Lean (lifted from so many different sources that no one remembers which ones) is "Getting the right things to the right place at the right time in the right quantity, while minimizing waste and being flexible and open to change."

We must warn you that Lean will succeed only with a complete top-down commitment from the leader of the enterprise. It is not a shortcut, a trend, or a silver bullet. For a social enterprise, it represents a total commitment to not externalizing waste and to eliminating it altogether. It means placing customer value and mission value at the center of everything that the enterprise does. And it means constant, relentless change that will energize some people and scare the daylights out of others. (See chapter 6; hire the kind it will energize!)

■ **PRACTITIONER'S TIP**
Lean is simple. But first, it's complicated.

To simplify the complicated part of Lean, go out and spend a few dollars on some of the resources that are readily available. Lean is a workbook lover's, diagram-and-flow-chart junkie's dream. Google "Lean manufacturing" to find dozens of quick and easy hands-on tools to help you turn our generalizations into tools you can work with.

A handful of Lean tools exist that any social enterprise will benefit from, whether manufacturing, retail, or service businesses. (We'll use the language of manufacturing companies, since that's what Rebuild and Greyston are, but the concepts are universal.) They are

- *Value-stream mapping*: Diagramming the value-added and non-value-added flow of all that you do
- *Kaizen*: Gaining wisdom from change
- *5S*: Removing the clutter under which waste hides, by sorting, stabilizing, shining, standardizing, and sustaining

Learn to use these Lean tools and you'll make great strides.

Value-Stream Mapping

Value-stream mapping is the core Lean process that precedes all the others. For a traditional business, it is a matter of identifying, measuring, diagramming, and flowing all of the tasks, both value-added and non-value-added, that bring the product all the way from raw material to the customer's hands. For a social enterprise, value-stream mapping also involves every activity that adds to or detracts from mission delivery. The process uses a simple but specific language and set of symbols to represent various aspects of the value stream. It places equal emphasis on identifying where value is created and identifying where it is not. It starts with a description of how things are now (often called the "current-state map") and then progresses to a description of how things should be in a world where waste has been eliminated (the "future-state map"). The gaps between current and future state become the focus of a continuous series of Lean projects.

Value-stream mapping can be done at the macro level of an organization as a whole or at the micro level of a division, a department, a product line, or even a single manufacturing line. Consider using it at a micro level first to produce immediate gains that will create belief and buy-in. Then roll it back to a macro view to identify priority targets. And then start knocking off the priority targets at a midview level for the long haul.

Some key concepts will come up time and time again in value-stream mapping. They are stated here from the perspective of a manufacturing environment but, with minimal modification, apply equally well to service and retail enterprises as well:

- Avoiding batch and queue production (which inevitably creates overproduction) in favor of continuous flow
- Using cellular thinking, which shortens production lines and sequences and replaces them with discrete, interchangeable, movable production functions
- Reducing changeover time by rethinking design and machine sequence issues
- Taking on the discipline of a FIFO (first in, first out) system to avoid obsolescence, waste, and deterioration

Kaizen

Lean is full of wonderful Japanese words like *hejunka*, *muda*, and our personal favorite, *poka-yoke*. Let's concentrate on perhaps the most important, *Kaizen*. This is a combination of two terms: *kai*, which means "to change," and *zen*, "to gain wisdom from doing." Put them together, and you're talking about *gaining wisdom from change*.

Kaizen picks up where your value-stream mapping left off. In the mapping process you identify the gaps between the current state and the idealized future state. Those gaps become grist for the mill of an endless series of incremental, worker-led improvements. What makes this process Kaizen, not just *kai*, is the emphasis on constancy that is implied by continual wisdom gaining. In other words, the process that was just improved is now exposed as something that can and should be improved again, and what is learned in improving it can also be used to improve dozens of other processes.

As the leader of a social enterprise, you may particularly appreciate the democratic, grassroots nature of Kaizen. To carry it off, you must respect your workers' abilities to spot problems and be willing to release their innate capacity to fix them. Your emphasis is on making small improvements all the time, which will accumulate to become large systemic changes. You must focus on the improvement, not the source. A good idea for a small change recognizes neither rank nor hierarchy. All that matters is the change, the waste it drives out, and the further wisdom it produces.

Lean companies reject the traditional thinking of "if it ain't broke, don't fix it" and replace it with the Kaizen philosophy of "do it better, make it better, improve it even if it ain't broken, because if we don't, we can't compete with those who do."[3]

Only a company with a healthy culture can produce a bountiful Kaizen harvest. If you are unwilling to be the kind of leader who creates an atmosphere of honesty and humility where everyone can freely admit problems, if your ego precludes a collaborative environment where value is placed not on the source of an idea but only on the idea itself, or if you are not personally passionate about producing value for the customer and the common good, Kaizen cannot succeed.

If you embrace Kaizen, it will help you create the healthy culture you crave.

5S

5S derives from a Japanese concept of housekeeping. The fundamental idea is that waste hides beneath clutter and can be eliminated only when the clutter is removed. 5S is a systematic way to remove clutter and keep it from reappearing so that inconspicuous waste becomes exposed to the light of day. Here are the steps you will take in that process, whether for an area, a department, or a whole plant:

1. *Sort* everything out into three groups: what you will retain, what you will return elsewhere, and what you will get rid of.
2. *Stabilize* whatever you will retain so that, in the words of your mother, there is a place for everything, and everything in its place.
3. *Shine* the entire area with a deep clean. You'll be amazed what it does for attitudes, for your ability to spot malfunctioning gear, and for worker safety.
4. *Standardize/systematize* schedules and systems of regulation to maintain the stable and shiny state you've created.
5. *Sustain* the culture through enforcements, consequences, and reinforcement.

The Lean Social Enterprise

Remember, you're not just a manufacturing, retailing, or service company in the widget business. You're in the business of widgets *and the common good*.

Your mission delivery might be harder to Lean than your core business processes if for no other reason than that your mission is probably more subtle, qualitative, and difficult to measure. It may even be counterintuitive to *want* to Lean it. For example, many social enterprises (including both Greyston and Rebuild) deliver their missions by employing people. You might worry that Lean will make you so efficient as to require fewer workers, thereby reducing your mission delivery.

That's a terrible trap you must avoid. Your enterprise cannot succeed without relentlessly focusing on customer value.

■ PRACTITIONER'S TIP

If creating customer value conflicts with mission delivery, improve mission delivery.

Rebuild Resources' core process is to take in the raw material of recovering people who want to put their lives back together and produce sober people who are capable of holding a job and becoming self-sufficient. For Rebuild, success means that someone gets a job elsewhere and leaves Rebuild. It also means that Rebuild loses a good worker, which wreaks havoc with production.

A few years back, Rebuild reviewed its mission delivery results and noticed that, over the course of time, people were getting stuck and not leaving the Rebuild program long after they were ready because it was too comfortable for them to stay. Rebuild set out to Lean its program side. It set a limit on the program length, which gave people a firm deadline by which they had to find a job. It added all sorts of coaching and job-search training to give people the tools with which to move on. It created an evaluation process that let them see their progress at every step. And most importantly, it created an orientation process at the front end so that they would understand from day one that their main job was to leave.

It was no coincidence that Rebuild was doing all of this at the same time that it was getting deeply into Lean work on the production floor. And a funny thing happened. Despite higher turnover, Rebuild created more value for its customers because the workforce became more vital, engaged, and committed. And it created more value for the community because Rebuild placed many more graduates.

One of the core premises of this book is the need to take social enterprises to scale so that we can collectively create the common good on the massive scale these times require. If we cannot get our "little" social enterprises to operate at the highest possible levels of quality, productivity, efficiency, and customer value, they will remain just that: little social enterprises, spread all across the land, tapping little markets of sympathizers and fighting merely to sustain themselves.

That's not what the authors signed up for. We're pretty sure it's not what our readers signed up for either. Scale enterprises require scale thinking, and that means competing with the best traditional businesses in our industries.

■ PRACTITIONER'S TIP
Scale thinking requires a fierce commitment to operational excellence.

We leave this topic with an anecdote from Darell Hammond that sums it all up:

I remember in the early days of KaBOOM! we were working with Home Depot. There was a problem in a project in Vancouver, and the head of community relations called me and told me about the problem. I jumped on a plane. We solved the problem, and I can still remember Saturday night after the playground was built, leaving her a message saying, "Problem solved. I was there. No problem." She called me on Monday morning and said, "You know, you don't get it. The issue is, if you have to jump on a plane, there must be something wrong with your processes or checks and balances. It's not scalable because it needs to be dependent on you."

And it was a humbling moment in time to say that the systems and the processes have to be as great and as

significant as the people, that if anything ever happens to
you it can outlive and scale beyond what one person is
capable of doing.[4]

Darell Hammond is not a small man. But he is Lean.

Metrics versus instinct

MEASURING SUCCESS

You can tell an awful lot about a business by what and how it measures. So to distinguish between a social enterprise and a non-social enterprise, you need look no further than the key reported metrics. In an NSE, the metrics are almost entirely financial. First among these is the measurement of market capitalization.

In a social enterprise, financial results are also reported, but these metrics are reported *in relationship to* the measurements of social impact that go to the core purpose of creating the common good.

To be clear, an NSE might also collect and report certain metrics around its social impact. Target Corporation, for example, has a huge strategy around community philanthropy. It measures every dollar it gives to every group at every location and proudly displays signs in every store meticulously describing how much money it has given away and to whom. All of this makes an impact in its communities. It has every right to trumpet that impact in its in-store marketing campaigns. But the fact that Target collects and reports that information does not make it a social enterprise.

■ **UNLOCKING THE EIGHTH PARADOX**

Your business isn't a social enterprise until you can prove it with blended social and financial metrics.

Are people's careers going to be made on, are their raises and bonuses going to be tied to, is the board's evaluation of management going to be based on the financial metrics, the social metrics, or the blended metrics? If the answer is the financial metrics, you're a for-profit NSE. If the answer is the social metrics, you're a nonprofit NSE. If the answer is the blended metrics, welcome to the club! You *are* a social enterprise, regardless of whether you happen to have the tax status of a nonprofit or a for-profit.

Why Bother?

You know that you're making a difference in the world and you have plenty of supporters who also take it as an article of faith that you're doing so. Given the time, money, and attention that building good systems for measuring social impact takes, you might be tempted to avoid the topic altogether. REDF, widely considered the thought leader in the entire field of measuring social enterprise impact, understands the temptation. REDF's Cynthia Gair puts it rather bluntly:

> There is this dilemma: do you want to pour all the money into measuring, when that money could probably do quite a bit toward actually helping people *do* things? It's sort of a quandary about where to put your money . . . We value measurement of outcomes, but most important to us is helping people move along in their lives and move out of their difficult situation.[1]

Why put your energy into an activity that is not directly producing results? Because you want *better* results, that's why. Just as production-floor metrics improve the processes in your factories, social-impact metrics help you find better, faster, more efficient ways to deliver to the world what it needs from you. You measure what is important. If it is not measured, it is likely not something that you are trying to improve.

But beware to never collect social metrics in a vacuum. Instead, take the artful approach of collecting them and reporting them right alongside your financials. In fact, you'll generally find a direct and traceable relationship between social impacts and financial impacts. Your ability to carve out true costs on both sides of the equation will improve each and every decision in your enterprise.

If you remain unconvinced, then consider another argument for investing in measurement systems: the rapid emergence of capital markets for social enterprise. This is great news for any enterprise that hopes to go to scale. But remember, sophisticated sources of expansion capital have the know-how and, frankly, the fiduciary duty to deploy capital where it will have the greatest blended social and financial return. Fail to develop credible metrics and these markets will leave you behind.

■ PRACTITIONER'S TIP
Measure impact to improve it.

By the very nature of what it is you're trying to measure-to-improve, you're facing a tricky measurement and reporting challenge, made all the more difficult by the newness of the field of social impact reporting. Think about it. Going way back in time to Pacioli's invention of double-entry bookkeeping, financial reporting has never had to change much. Virtually any company can be lined up next to any other company or set of companies and be compared on the same handful of key ratios and indicators. Not so with the nascent field of social enterprises.

It's really not very hard to set up good financial measurements. An entire set of GAAP (generally accepted accounting principles) has been devised to standardize how it's done. Get a reasonably decent piece of enterprise software or stick with an old-fashioned columnar pad and you're in business, whether your business is McDonald's, Boeing, or the corner grocery.

On the other hand, every social enterprise is different. The common good is a vast goal toward which to aspire. Everybody who is working toward it is working on a different part. If you're going to claim progress—and you must, for many reasons—you must be clear, from the outset, about what you really want to have happen in the world because of the existence of your enterprise.

■ **PRACTITIONER'S TIP**
Build common-good measurements, from the ground up, into the front end of the enterprise.

Here are just a few examples of what our colleagues are measuring, or at least attempting to measure:

- *At Give Something Back*: Percent of accumulated retained earnings given away via philanthropic dollars (a whopping 78 percent, to date, according to Mike Hannigan!).[2]
- *At Seventh Generation*: Product efficaciousness of no less than 90 percent of that of the leading product in each category, and superiority from health and environmental standpoints to *all* products in the category. (What makes this an

interesting approach to measurement is that measurements are made only in relation to other products that represent the status quo Seventh Generation is seeking to alter.)[3]

- *Also at Seventh Generation:* The size of the category in which the product competes. (This is a very sophisticated way to look at social purpose, which allows a small impact on a big problem to count as much as a bigger impact on a smaller problem.)[4]

- *At Benetech's BookShare.org enterprise* (a web-based system supplying accessible books in digital formats for people with disabilities): Number of users, subscription renewal rates, number of downloads, number of books in the collection, number of books scanned by volunteers.[5]

- *At Benetech's Martus enterprise* (an open-source software system for ensuring that the documentation of human-rights violations is safeguarded and disseminated): Number of bulletins and number of server backups.[6]

- *At KaBOOM!:* "Value," the number of kids served in low-income communities, as defined by reduced-cost or free lunch programs, and the square footage of space being developed into play space; "efficiency," dollars raised, contracts executed, and volunteers engaged; and "leverage and amplification," the rate at which volunteers become longer-term advocates and partners.[7]

- *At Guayaki:* Amount of rainforest reforestation, species per hectare, and number of acres preserved and dedicated to sustainably harvested mate.[8]

- *At TROSA* (and coincidentally, at Rebuild as well): Percentage of program participants who graduate and placement rate of graduates. Also at TROSA, GEDs attained and drivers' licenses obtained.[9]

- *At Calvert Foundation* (relative to the lending it does to other social enterprises): Number of housing units produced, number of child-care slots created, number of jobs created, and square footage of commercial construction. (Notably, in these measurements, Calvert recognizes it is really measuring "output," not true social impact, since the social impact is created, in turn, by the organizations to which it lends.)[10]

- *At Greyston*: Good turnover (when employees leave for a career or job opportunity that better fits their lives) versus bad turnover (when an employee is asked to leave or leaves without having a better job opportunity lined up).

To our knowledge, the prize for state-of-the-art measurement systems for social impact goes to Rubicon, whose CICERO system has been widely lauded as the best of field. What is impressive about CICERO is not just its technological platform for capturing and reporting data but the nuanced approach to true social impact that it presents. Rick Aubry explains that CICERO measures all of the interactions between Rubicon and those it serves so that Rubicon can evaluate the impact of programs and combinations of programs on achieving its common-good goal of moving people from poverty to sustainability:

> If you roll it up to three of the most important things that we look for, we sort of compare the income of people when they walk in our door to where they are at six months, a year, and two years down the line to see if there is in fact both job creation and wage growth over that period of time . . . Since a significant number of people we serve were homeless when they walked in our door, we compare their housing stability at the point of entry to six months, a year, and two years down the line. We

also measure involvement in the criminal justice system as at least a proxy for cost savings that we are creating and impact on people's lives. In some programs that, for example, are targeted at fathers, we monitor the child-support payment that the dads do at entry versus further on, their engagement with the lives of their young children, as well as the job and housing stability that they have. So a very significant amount of resources is invested in measurement of the impact that we have, and it is published and available on our web site for investors to see.[11]

If a Tree Falls in the Woods but There's No One Around to Hear It

A good leader, when faced with a tough decision, collects input and information from as many sources as possible but never abdicates the duty of deciding. In the long, dark hours of the night, the courage to make a call and move on is what separates leader from follower.

So it is with the world of measurement.

As the list of items our colleagues are measuring bears out, you can and should measure plenty of things. By all reasonable means, go ahead and do so.

You may never be able to measure other things. "How do you mark down something about learning to care again, that there is hope?" asks Kevin McDonald.[12]

This is where faith, passion, and conviction come in. While business schools may try to beat common sense and intuition out of their graduates, we would argue that these soft skills are absolutely essential requirements for you as a social enterprise leader.

Use measurements to inform your instincts, not replace them.

Start with values. You will never, and we mean never *ever*, be able to quantify the social impact of love and compassion. Operate a loving and compassionate enterprise anyway. You can't measure what it means to treat your employees well, to be square with your customers, to pay your suppliers fairly and promptly. Do all of these anyway. And so on. Of course they have a cost to them. So what? If you're not willing to compromise about them, don't bother measuring them.

Outputs to Outcomes

We strive to change the world for the better. Let us not be so egotistical as to believe that we can control the entire set of variables necessary to do so. Even if we ever could, that which we seek to change would change before we could measure it.

That is why it is so important to be very clear about the difference between measuring outputs and measuring outcomes. Think, for example, about what it means to move out of poverty. REDF has researched this extensively as a key supporter of social enterprises working in this field. According to Cynthia Gair,

> We have positive [evidence] that if people get a job and increase their wages and span a job over two years, they are on the way to moving out of poverty. But assessing whether a person moves out of poverty permanently would take years of monitoring . . . We've found that just measuring longitudinally for two years after baseline is a pretty unusual thing in the world of social-science measuring.[13]

What we *can* do, or what we have to at least settle for, is to measure specific actions, aggregate these actions into movements, and then project the cumulative effect of these into ultimate outcomes. This is the heart of what has been termed the KaBOOM! formula, according to Darell Hammond:

> We manage outputs and occasionally do longitudinal studies on what are the outcomes that we are achieving. I think it is important to note that we manage outputs and occasionally outcomes because if we were constantly trying to measure outcomes, it would take seven to ten years for us to be looking at what those outcomes are, and by the time we tried to have process improvement, . . . it would be five years into a cycle. [So, for example,] an input is the number of people who are hitting our web site; an output is the number of people who are registering and then making posts, and an outcome is the number of people who actually go on to build [a community playground]. And if they build, do they have a higher degree of civic responsibility, do they go volunteer more frequently, are the kids more healthy? Those are outcomes.[14]

Just as importantly, consider the phenomenon of measuring what *doesn't* happen in the world because of your enterprise. That may be the ultimate measure of your impact—and the hardest of all to measure. It's a key measurement for Joan Pikas relative to the women escaping from poverty at The Enterprising Kitchen: "They may not necessarily leave here and be immediately employed. But if they don't lose their housing and they don't go back to jail and they keep on that positive path, then that is another measure of success."[15]

Remember, too, that this whole issue of measurement is a two-way street. It's not just about tracking what your enterprise is doing to improve a social condition. Flip it on its head once and you'll discover that it's also worth measuring what improving a social condition does to your enterprise. Basic market research and business analysis may very well prove that your enterprise's social impact is also serving your bottom line.

Build It In

When you're as focused as you must be on the day-to-day running of the business, it can be hard to find the bandwidth to do the kind of measurements you really should do. We have some simple suggestions that may help.

Most fundamentally, remember to think about social-impact measurement at the very earliest stages of your enterprise. You'll find it easier to collect the information you may need if you build the collection into every other system you use for managing the enterprise—and easier to track your progress if your baseline extends all the way to day one of your enterprise.

Internally, communicate and celebrate your social metrics frequently and regularly. Break the metrics into small chunks that can be measured quickly and easily and can be displayed visually in your workspaces. Nothing will motivate and unify your staff more than to see regular evidence of the impact they are having on the world.

Report social impact wherever and whenever you report financial information. If social results go hand in hand with financial results, one should never be displayed without the other. Include social metrics in your executive summaries, on dashboards, and in the financial reports themselves.

■ **PRACTITIONER'S TIP**
Measure frequently and regularly—
and celebrate results!

An interesting phenomenon develops when you do all of this measuring right. You'll find that your business partners become more interested in your social results, while your social partners become more interested in your business results. Some would call that a blended bottom line. We'd call it a good thing.

10

Growth versus focus
EXPANDING SENSIBLY

For most economists and business leaders, a single word defines success: "growth." At the very heart of the state religion that is our NSE-dominated economic system is a fundamental article of faith that states that gross national product (and its variants) must continuously increase.

In turn, the income statements and balance sheets of businesses must grow as well. Indeed, only through continuous growth can the relentless hunger of ownership be sated. As we proposed at the outset, the need for social enterprise—the very market opportunity, if you will—is borne in response to the fundamental social ills that are the unfortunate result of the single-minded focus on growth above all. If businesses were no longer driven, in their quest for continual growth, to off-load true costs onto society as a whole, there would be fewer environmental problems for Seventh Generation to reverse, less generational poverty for Rubicon to redress, fewer human-rights abuses for Benetech's software to track, and less pressure on the rainforest for Guayaki to preserve.

How, then, should a social enterprise consider the inevitable issues of growth and expansion? A traditional business need only follow its default instinct—grow!—and put its attention on how to do so at any cost. But a social enterprise must take one step back and ask a more fundamental question: *Why* grow?

■ UNLOCKING THE NINTH PARADOX
Avoid the seduction of growth for growth's sake. Grow *only* for the right reasons.

This is not the traditional world of business, where the guiding force is to increase shareholder value and enterprise growth is the Holy Grail.

Do you want to grow because, well, that's what businesses do? We humbly suggest that that is not a very good reason if you are leading a true social enterprise, even though it may feel like a biological imperative. If you find yourself on this path, you must quickly conduct a reality check with yourself and your stakeholders. Failure to do so can seduce you toward decisions that make it increasingly difficult to remember why you started your enterprise in the first place. Before you know it, you may find yourself no longer single-mindedly serving the common good. Growth decisions can be vastly different from mission decisions.

Are you expanding because you must, and if you don't, the enterprise will die? This is neither an uncommon nor an unreasonable explanation. Many businesses are forced to expand because their current revenue stream is insufficient to cover the underlying overhead expenses. If they don't expand they will either run out of resources through lost dollars on each sale of a product or service or, if they choose to raise prices, they will lose their customer base. Expanding to cover overhead is understandable; a certain level of critical mass is necessary to cover fixed costs and achieve sustainability. Beware that the need to act out of survival may lead to erroneous assumptions about the market. However, it can also rightly lead to a frank discussion about the current business model.

Or are you expanding because the social mission demands that you go to scale? In the long run, in our view, social impact is the *only* reason that is really worthy of the effort to grow. The current scale of social enterprise as a whole is not sufficient to make a big enough impact, fast enough, on behalf of the common good. Our enterprises need to expand not because we want bigger enterprises but because we want bigger impact. That's the point of a conversation Clara Miller frequently has with enterprises that come to her seeking expansion capital:

> Rapid growth is difficult and much more risky, and it produces all kinds of upheaval, from culture change to the need for much, much more money in various forms (especially cash). We all think that rapid growth is good, right? You're higher profile, you're doing more, you're serving more. We're all imagining that the more people we serve, the better off the world will be and the better off we will be financially. But that's the catch. We are almost always already doing something that produces tiny or negative margins. And those don't improve with growth but do require attention—increased efficiency, more fund-raising contributions, increased pricing, and sometimes all three. And the faster you go, the harder it is. For some business models that are not really scalable, growth will so greatly impair quality that it will come at the expense of mission effectiveness. And that's also very little understood. So, the first thing to do is to figure out how (or whether) growth will actually produce better social value.[1]

Greyston doesn't want to employ more people to make more brownies. It wants to make more brownies to employ more people. See the difference?

Grow What?

Two primary routes are available to a social enterprise that is ready and able, for all the right reasons, to expand its social impact through business growth. One way is to do more of the thing it does. The other is to do more things.

We can't tell you how many times we've met folks at social enterprise conferences who are running two or three separate, unrelated businesses within their organization and are thinking about adding a couple more. They are following the second route. Although we have not examined their success empirically, this approach seems fraught with difficulty.

We know of only a small handful of social enterprises with the bandwidth and capacity to even consider the conglomerate model of owning many different businesses. Even in the world of traditional businesses, we see large conglomerates exiting businesses that do not leverage their core competencies. Many years ago, a large salted-snack company announced its intention to take over the cookie business. It said, "We are great at making salted snacks. We can be great at making cookies." Hundreds of millions of dollars later, it wrote off its investment and is a bit player in the cookie business.

Unless you are running a ninety-nine-cent store, you cannot be "anything for a buck." It is impossible to drive business success when the focus is not on one reasonably defined product or service scope. The world today is too fluid to allow your business to be competitive at making crayons and doughnuts or at providing tax service and dentistry. The skill sets to be successful in those businesses are so particular as to not be transferable.

We are huge advocates of the first approach: become very, very good at our core business, constantly improving both how we serve the market and how we create social benefit through the business, and take *that* business to scale. Fail to do that, and all we will have done is create another whole bunch of little, inefficient, duplicative social enterprises tilting at windmills without making a substantive, sustainable impact on the common good.

If you are already spread thin in multiple enterprises, you may even find yourself in the position of having to exit existing businesses to grow the core. This is difficult at many levels, not the least of which is that of the organization's self-image and its leader's ego. A large number of the mistakes made regarding growth and expansion are driven by the blind need to not admit failure.

Both Greyston and Rebuild have found it necessary to "shrink to grow": Greyston, by getting out of the "fancy cake" business that had long been part of its self-identity, and Rebuild, by shedding three of its five businesses in 2006. For Lynch, this was one of the most painful and ego-bruising, but necessary, chapters in his career. Rebuild had literally stumbled into a collection of little enterprises that had each seemed like an opportunity when Rebuild first had got into them. Some years later, Lynch joined Rebuild. When he did, he came in with his chest puffed up, figuring he could get all of them firing on all cylinders. But once he was handling all of them, there was no way to give any of them the attention or resources they deserved. Lynch had never been so frustrated as a leader as when he realized after a couple of years that he was doing a lousy job on all of them. So he and his board did an objective analysis of which ones were both advancing the mission and creating some margins, and three of them could not be justified. He pulled the plug on those three. Probably the darkest day of his career was the day he had to tell the good people who were working in those enterprises that he was closing them down so Rebuild could survive. That was two years ago. Rebuild has had a lot more success and growth as a focused effort, but letting go of the people is something that still haunts him.

■ **PRACTITIONER'S TIP**
Do more of the thing you do, not more things.

Mission Creep

The term "mission creep" originated in the military to describe the all-too-common phenomenon of sending troops to do a job and then failing to notice as they slowly but surely get side-tracked—often for the best of reasons—to the point where they are no longer in position to complete the mission. This is the very opposite of recognizing that what you are trying to accomplish will no longer meet your needs or is no longer wanted in the market, or you simply can't carry it off. This is where the discipline of business shows up. Mission creep will kill your core business. It will drain your dollar and human resources into areas that simply suck energy from areas of more successful application of that energy.

To keep you and your organization focused, you need to draft some mission criteria—ones that do not easily bend in whichever direction the wind blows yet are flexible enough to allow you to incorporate your learnings as you progress along the business expansion process. Rick Aubry speaks of three criteria that Rubicon uses:

> They have evolved over time, but now basically there are three criteria . . . and they are all mission driven. First and foremost, does it create jobs that are a benefit to the peo-

ple that we serve? So the nature of the work, the wages of the work, the ability of the work to lead to jobs in other industries, living wages, internal growth within the business, career ladders are all criteria that are considered. That's one of the legs of the stool. The second leg is the business itself. Is it the kind of business that could succeed? Are the sources of capital available to Rubicon? Is there a business plan that shows that there is some sort of competitive advantage that will lead us to believe that it is going to succeed as a business? The third leg of the stool is the overall fit of the business with the brand image of Rubicon. Is it a business that we would want to be associated with? So those are the criteria.[2]

In summary, these are the key criteria for evaluating an expansion opportunity:

- Does it produce measurable mission outputs?
- Can you succeed at the business?
- Does it fit your brand image?

One Basket, Too Many Eggs

Paradoxically, it is possible to be *too* focused. As we discussed in chapter 4 on planning, you need to remain ever available to the possibility that the universe is going to hand you an opportunity that defies everything you have learned about discipline and single-mindedness.

Now, if you're doing a great job with your product and with your marketing, you may wake up one day with another kind of potential problem. It's a good problem and one that any enterprise without it would love to have: the mixed blessing of a *big gorilla customer*. That's that single customer with the kind of volume requirement that can put you on the map, absorb a huge portion of your overhead, justify substantial overhead or personnel investments, and spell the difference between profit and loss.

According to Scott Leonard, landing that kind of customer was a profound turning point for Indigenous Designs: "In 1995 we got our first big break. We were asked to produce nine thousand units for The Nature Company in a single order and we had to produce them in a 120-day window, with all of them having quality control. It was a reference product, a $450K purchase order, and a landmark for the company."[3]

But that same big customer can also keep you awake at night. Last year, Joan Pikas did a lot of business with a very large retail apparel company that was buying The Enterprising Kitchen's products as a gift-with-purchase item and as an employee gift. The company put in several large orders, a primary reason that sales went up. But, says Pikas, "My fear is that they will decide, maybe not this year but maybe next year, that they may want to do some other gift-with-purchase item that's not soap and go to another very worthwhile organization. So you can't put all your eggs in one basket."[4]

We daresay that this is a universal problem for just about every social enterprise that has made it, or is going to make it, to scale. You can choose from two equally valid ways to deal with it.

The first may be painful and counterintuitive, and it will take a great deal of courage and intellectual honesty to carry out: turn down the customer. If you are not convinced that you can figure out a way to deliver in every way—without driving past your headlights—then you need to take a deep breath, say no, and go immediately to work fixing the parts of your enterprise that were not ready for Mr. Big. We guarantee the customer will respect you today. And we *almost* guarantee that the customer will give you another shot in the future or give you a piece of business on which you *can* succeed.

The second solution is a little bit more fun and a lot more work: take on the customer, pull out all the stops to deliver, *and immediately go out and find two or three more customers just like it.* But before you make this decision, have a frank conversation with the customer to assess the following:

- Why are they buying from you?
- Do they just want a competitive product or service? Or is there something about your product or service and mission that matches theirs, thereby motivating them to buy from you?
- Does your mission bring them some goodwill in the market?
- How long are they committed to you as their supplier?
- Is this a one-time purchase?
- Can you secure a contract for a specific time frame or dollar value?
- Are they buying similar products from another supplier?
- Are you the primary or the backup supplier?
- If you are the backup supplier, do you have an opportunity to become the primary supplier?
- Who is making the change decision? How will it be made?
- How much notice will you have when the partnership ends?

These aren't just good business questions but business questions that help you assess the impact the relationship and its eventual dissolution may have on your social mission. A good partner will appreciate the conversation and have a very similar set of concerns of its own. The one who won't engage frankly in this discussion is the one with whom you don't want to get into bed.

Begin replacing the big customer the moment you land it.

What It Takes to Grow and Expand

Given a thorough understanding of why you seek to grow, a thorough commitment to growing in a focused and disciplined manner, and a clear vision of the balance between mission creep and concentration of risk, you can now go merrily on your ever-expanding way. Or can you? You still need to have a few more essential ingredients in place:

- Market opportunity
- Resources, financing, and capacity
- Culture
- Discipline
- Leadership

Market Opportunity

Focused growth starts with answering the question, Is your model scalable? That is, *can* it be expanded? You need intellectual discipline and honesty to answer this objectively. Be careful to not get confused between *your need* to expand the business and the *marketplace need* for your expanded business. This question must be answered from the critical view of

- Do we have a product or service the market can use more of?
- Do we have a service or product the market wants in addition to what we already offer?

The market is unforgiving. It will let you know that your product or service is not needed at all or in any additional quantity. Be certain to get in touch with what the market needs when determining if you will expand.

Many businesspeople have the illusion that they do not have any competitors. They assume that if they increase their capacity to service or produce, the market will emerge to absorb that capacity. For example, at first glance, Greyston Bakery has no competitor in the nationally branded premium brownie market. There are a number of regionally distributed brands but none nationally. However, everyone that markets a dessert item is a competitor. Greyston competes against other sweet baked goods such as cookies and cakes, against every ice cream manufacturer, and against every candy manufacturer. In some homes, a brownie will even compete with fruit for the dessert spot on the table.

A business must humbly compare its product or service to any and all possible competitors. If it does not, it may misread a void in the marketplace or find itself blindsided by competition that it is ill-prepared to handle. Remember, the results of a miscalculation are doubly severe for a social enterprise: your risk capital is more precious, and what the world needs you to accomplish on its behalf is greater.

Resources, Financing, and Capacity

You have decided you have a product or service of which the market wants more than you are currently supplying. Now you must learn how, responsibly, within your means, to meet that demand. Can you actually meet the demands of the customer if it gives you that large order? Customers like nothing less than being promised a product or service that doesn't materialize. They want the product or service when they want it. Your late delivery isn't what they want. They can get that elsewhere. It is better to forgo the large customer now and attempt to secure it later than to secure the order and then lose it. Customers have bad memories for good things but great memories for bad things.

Even if you gather every possible resource to support your expansion, you can become so overleveraged that if a particular expansion strategy doesn't work, you are in trouble. If you are attempting an expansion from the standpoint of "expand or die," you may not care about the consequences of failure because this is the potential consequence that is steering you to expand in the first place. That is a reasonable logic stream, but please consider that a prolonged failure is more excruciating than a swift one and may be a worse use of resources than allowing someone else to fill your place in the market.

A lack of resources may cause you to think with the same poverty mind-set we cautioned about earlier. You might use lesser-quality materials because you are stretched too thin. You might make a sale but fail to make the customer a repeat customer or, worse yet, induce the customer to tell others about the bad quality of product or service received from you. You might reduce your marketing budget below the proper percentage allocation for your market and go unnoticed, saving marketing dollars, but dooming your product for lack of exposure. You might pay less than a competitor, saving labor dollars in the short term but eventually losing your best employees or, worst of all, losing them *and* the customers they take with them.

In addition, a lack of resources may trick you into being more conservative in the marketplace than is necessary to achieve success. You may have some of the resources, but if you don't have what is necessary to do a job right, don't do it at all. Wait. Wait until you get the resources. This, too, is a tough discipline, but remember once again that the market is unrelenting. It will not prop you up and take care of you until you are ready. You must be mature enough in resources to grow up in the market. A lack of resources will drive you to make mistakes on product or service decisions. You will make mission-adverse decisions. You will not shoulder your basic responsibility to live to fight another day.

Culture

The greatest of ideas with the most abundant of resources will fail if the culture is not conducive to success. You will want to be proactive in establishing your culture such that it is aligned with your mission, objectives, and the message you want to deliver through your marketing.

The moment of growth and expansion is not when you should begin to think about culture. For better or for worse, you have been building a culture all along. The atmosphere, the interpersonal relationships, the individual personalities, and the business needs have all been coming together, since day one and maybe even before, to create your culture. It may or may not be the culture you want.

We could have put this section on culture in several different locations in this book. We chose to put it here for one simple reason: *the moment of growth and expansion is when your culture will be most put to the test.*

Your employees contribute to the culture and are impacted by it. They will adapt to the culture of the place or be miserable. If they fail to adapt, they'll leave or make the rest of the place miserable, thereby creating a new culture of miserable people. Miserable people are viral. They infect the rest of your staff. Miserable people do not perform well, no matter what you ask them to do. Ask them to go beyond the status quo, as is necessary during expansion, and you are sunk.

Your *only* choice is to create a healthy culture. In chapter 6, we spoke of four practices for improving the life of the people in your organization: aspiration, say, voice, and ritual. These practices are the building blocks of a healthy culture for your enterprise. As you add more people during this expansionary time, you must attend to these practices constantly.

- With regard to *aspiration*, recognize that "going for it," in the big way you now intend, is an enormous amount of work and risk. It also gives people something new toward which to aspire. Harness that energy around the greater social impact your growing enterprise will create.
- Growth and expansion require vision, discipline, and innovation, all within an environment requiring quick and facile decision making. Giving *say* in this environment is more important than ever, although your temptation may be to do everything yourself.
- The burgeoning enterprise has more points of contact with more stakeholders than ever before. Here again, awarding *voice* to as many employees as possible allows you to effectively present the organization at *every* point of contact.
- And finally, don't forget to make time for *ritual*. Working at the speed of growth makes this practice the easiest to leave by the wayside. Do you *really* have time to start each meeting with a moment of silence (if that is one of your rituals) when you are at warp speed? You don't have time *not* to!

Discipline

If you are expanding because your business is doing well, the discipline of market examination is still important. Act aggressively but responsibly. Don't become reckless just because things are going well *now*. Follow the biblical principle of Joseph and save for a drought. Things do not always go well. Create a reserve fund that will be available if—strike that, *when*—things go wrong.

Once you have asked the questions and answered them honestly and without the blindness of personal or corporate ego, return to the principles of chapter 4 and put them down on paper in the form of a business plan. Don't make the fatal mistake of not following the discipline of planning because "this is just an expansion." This expansion needs and deserves every opportunity to succeed, just like your start-up did. Failing to plan is planning to fail. It is not just a cliché. It is Business Start-Up 101 and Business Expansion 102.

Leadership

Another kind of discipline is perhaps more important than anything else we've touched on in the area of growth and expansion. This is your discipline as a leader. More specifically, it is your attention to how you gather your own capabilities and resources to lead the organization through this phase. Discipline is far from easy as the excitement of growth, the demands on your skills, and the toll on your energy and your own ego all collide. Take none of this for granted. It is so critically important to your enterprise's health that we've devoted the entire following chapter to it.

11

Sweat equity versus blood equity

CARING FOR YOURSELF

We know from parents, school, and a lifetime of societal messages that we need to contribute, sacrifice, and drive hard in order to achieve success. We have been taught all along that we will have to invest in our own success.

In the business world, when dollars are invested in the starting of a business, it's called equity. Another type of equity is called sweat equity. Sweat equity accrues when someone puts in time and effort for no immediate compensation but is a contributor to the success of a business and will be rewarded for this sweat with a share in the success of the business when the equity is sold or pays dividends. Many times this equity goes unrewarded because many businesses fail. The investment of sweat equity is an understood risk for the possibility of a high return.

But what if your contribution to the enterprise goes beyond sweat equity? What if the effort goes beyond a reasonable investment of time? What if the exertion of effort is more than sweat? What if the toll of this unusually high contribution on your part starts to impact your health? What if this begins to negatively impact your relationship with your spouse and children?

We call this blood equity. It's what you give when you have no more sweat equity to give. You are in danger of having life's blood sapped out of you. You are at risk of contributing until you have nothing left to contribute. It is precisely because social enterprise is rewarding in so many ways beyond financial that we need to be on guard about allowing that to happen. As you do your very needed work, you must be diligent not to allow all of the pressures of completing your mission and running a successful business to drive you to contribute more than sweat.

Symptoms of blood equity include lack of time at home, lack of being fully present when you *are* at home, and constant attention to your BlackBerry when you're out. It shows up as constant multitasking; curtailment of hobbies and social life; sleep deprivation; increased use of drugs, alcohol, and food; or decreased interest in sex.

■ UNLOCKING THE TENTH PARADOX
Accept the sweat, but draw the line at your blood and your family's tears.

Of course your work is going to stay on your mind. You're going to be thinking of how to position that next initiative or fill that rush order or make that key hire. All are very valid concerns. But when they start to negatively impact your relationship with your partner and children you must ask if that is acceptable.

You are a shepherd of a large and important calling. But your *life* is also a calling. To respond to both callings you will need to pay attention. You will either be lifted up or torn down. We've seen it go both ways.

The Right Stuff

You will need to take proactive steps to be able to successfully, and with grace and joy, handle all that will come at you because you have chosen to operate a social enterprise. Do you have what it takes? According to the Schwab Foundation for Social Entrepreneurship, the common traits of great social entrepreneurs include

- An unwavering belief in the innate capacity of all people to contribute meaningfully to economic and social development.
- A driving passion to make that happen.
- A practical but innovative stance to a social problem, often using market principles and forces, coupled with dogged determination, that allows them to break away from constraints imposed by ideology or field of discipline, and pushes them to take risks that others wouldn't dare.
- A zeal to measure and monitor their impact. Entrepreneurs have high standards, particularly in relation to their own organization's efforts and in response to the communities with which they engage. Data, both quantitative and qualitative, are their key tools, guiding continuous feedback and improvement.
- A healthy impatience. Social entrepreneurs don't do well in bureaucracies. They cannot sit back and wait for change to happen—they are the change drivers.[1]

If you're already in it with both feet, it may seem a bit too late to ask yourself if you have the right stuff. You probably wouldn't have made it this far if you don't. But note especially well the fourth point on the Schwab list—the one about monitoring your impact and seeking continuous improvement—and apply this principle to your own leadership. Measure yourself against the best in the field to continuously get better.

In this spirit, we offer you a collection of advice on maintaining joy, becoming continuously better, and ensuring the survival of the mission. This body of advice was repeated in one form or another by nearly every practitioner who lent wisdom to this volume. Therefore, it is important enough to warrant an entire baker's dozen of practitioner's tips.

Thirteen Tips for Taking Care of Yourself

Be conscious about the opportunity cost of doing something or not doing something. Just as every enterprise decision is a balance between mission and margin, your entire life as a leader requires that you make a conscious decision about what price you are willing to pay for your particular enterprise's success. Reduce the sweat-equity-versus-blood-equity dilemma to a specific, case-by-case decision-making process and keep track of it in written, quantitative terms if you have to: "If I do A, I can't do B. What is the impact on the business of not doing A? What is the impact on my family of not doing B? If I don't do A, how can I offset the impact of that on the business? If I don't do B, when and how can I restore the impact of that to the family?"

You measure your enterprise's financial well-being and social impact. Why not also measure its impact on your life?

■ PRACTITIONER'S TIP
Constantly measure and evaluate your balance point.

How much time will you spend daily, weekly, or monthly operating your enterprise? What time limits have you set for the business? Will you bring work home on some nights, every night, for special projects only, or never? Will you take business calls at night at home? Will you use personal resources, beyond any personal equity committed, to reach success? Will you mix vacation time and business trips? Only you can set these boundaries and then hold yourself to them. But do it before you are in the throes of crisis. That is not where we do our best thinking.

■ PRACTITIONER'S TIP
Set boundaries.

No matter how smart you think you are, how great a product or service you offer, or how compelling your social impact, you will experience times when things are not going well. You must plan for these times in advance.

Consider the following scenario. Before leaving your office for an important sales call, you learn you do not have enough money in your bank account to cover payroll. How do you prepare yourself to arrive not simply in a satisfactory emotional state but with an upbeat attitude that will translate into a confident presentation to that prospective customer? This is when you will have to fall back on your passion for the work. This is when you will need to be resilient. This is when, in the words of Kevin McDonald, you'll need to "bounce back from when they knock you on your ass."[2]

What is it that *you* need to pick yourself up when you're feeling low? This is something you will need to learn about yourself. Find out what works for you. Is it listening to a song that lifts you? Praying, if you are a praying person? Getting some exercise or getting into nature?

Know where you are going to go for a lift when those tough times come upon you.

■ PRACTITIONER'S TIP
You will have setbacks. Plan for them.

All of us should be in constant learning mode, but this is even more critical for social enterprise leaders. Your margin of error is thinner; quick recovery from a mistake may be the difference between a train wreck and a mere bump in the road. Launching that undesired product may cost money, but staying with it will sink the company. Hiring that untrustworthy manager may bring down morale, but not firing him or her will bring down the company. You will make mistakes. Searching for them and recovering from them will turn them into opportunities.

Don't get paralyzed by your mistakes. Most are neither as bad nor as long impacting as they feel in the moment. You can recover. Recognize the issue, develop options, and then make adjustments. Keep moving. Don't get stuck. Above all, avoid the blame game. Right there in the moment is not the time to figure out who is to blame. What matters now is moving the company forward. You will have ample time to reflect on what happened later. Assign responsibility for improving the company rather than assigning blame.

■ PRACTITIONER'S TIP
Learn from mistakes.

Be stingy with blame and generous with your own accountability. Learn from your mistakes and allow others to learn from them as well. You must first admit that you make mistakes. As Jeff Hollender puts it, "You need a hunger for your own growth and a humbleness that does not let what you know get in the way of what you do not know."[3]

If you are capable of admitting you are wrong, you give your people the gift and the freedom to admit when they have done something wrong. This cleanses their souls and promotes their emotional health. It allows for correction rather than cover-up. It leads to growth rather than stymied progress due to a lack of awareness of repeated mistakes and missteps. Mistakes are guideposts along the way to success. If you and your team can read them—and a requirement of reading them is becoming aware of them—you can take corrective action as you navigate the path to success.

■ PRACTITIONER'S TIP
Allow others to learn from your mistakes.

In the words of the inimitable Kevin McDonald: "Hey, sometimes things are not going to go like you think. So be able to switch gears, maybe go in another direction. It might be a little out of the way, but do that. Be innovative, man!"[4]

While business plans are necessary, they do not run your business. They are useful tools that provide benchmarks so that you can know when you are on track or off track. If you get off track, quickly assess why. Is the business making and delivering its product well? Is the market message on point? Is the market simply saying it doesn't want that service or product? Is your staff productive? Are you leading effectively?

You, as the entrepreneur, must read these tea leaves and respond. You must display a proper level of firmness so that any blowing wind does not move you and your organization. Your staff needs a firm focus and direction to be effective. But you also must not be so rigid that you bang your organization's head against the wall when the tea leaves have said no. Your judgment in this area will be one of the major keys to your organization's success. Hold firm to your vision and dream, but be flexible on its form.

■ PRACTITIONER'S TIP
Stretch out. Be flexible.

A very common breed of entrepreneurs and other leaders, particularly in this social-mission world, are the caretakers of all but themselves. This is a different conversation than the one about balancing work and family. Here we're talking about balancing "all"—including the business, the family, the community, the political activism, perhaps an aging parent or two—on one side of the scale against little old "you" on the other.

Be certain to schedule time away from everything and everyone to reflect on your personal health, which includes your spiritual well-being, your emotional health, your intellectual growth, and your physical condition. "Time away" means just that. Disconnect yourself from all the multiple ways in which you can be reached. At one hotel in the Midwest, you can check your cell phone and BlackBerry at the front desk to ensure you get a sane dinner and a good night's sleep. For the good of your health you must take time out to recuperate. You're not a good leader if your team can't get along without you, and you're not a good partner or parent if your family can't do the same.

■ PRACTITIONER'S TIP
Care for yourself.

Ask nothing of your staff that you wouldn't demand of yourself, including the demand for self-care. If you don't love the wonderful people with whom you are creating the common good enough to insist on their self-care, then you need to take a good look at your motivations. Maybe you really *don't* belong in this job.

■ PRACTITIONER'S TIP
Make sure your staff are taking care of themselves.

Find a simple, compelling way to articulate to yourself and demonstrate, through your actions, exactly what you stand for as a leader. For example, stand for the "Three Cs": clarity, consistency, and compassion.

Clarity of purpose allows you to focus on that single aim. You may have to complete many tasks to accomplish that aim, but knowing that single aim will drive you through many obstacles. Clarity of purpose will allow others to not just complete their tasks but participate with you in using the cumulative impact of all those tasks to create the common good.

Consistency brings credibility. The lack of it breeds contempt. People are watching your purpose-driven business to see if your values are consistent with your behaviors. You may be hiring a certain population and be applauded for that, but people will watch to see if you recycle. You may be a global supplier of wind energy, but people will want to know how you treat the community in which your business resides. You may do all these things, but your employees will want to know if you regard them as your most important asset and treat them in that manner.

Compassion is the humane quality of understanding the suffering of others and wanting to do something about it. Almost by definition, you cannot be in this business without this quality. If you lack it, that will show up. People will come to know you as doing this just for a buck.

■ PRACTITIONER'S TIP
Have a personal management philosophy.

It is your responsibility to set the tone and seed the creation of the culture of your organization. As the leader of a social enterprise, you want your culture driven by mission. Do not allow your organization's culture and mission to be in any way misaligned with how you live your own life, or you will not be able to fulfill your mission. For example, Lynch is a recovering addict and alcoholic, with fourteen years of sobriety under his belt, leading an organization with a recovery mission. If he took even one drink, he could no longer be credible as Rebuild's leader. He would have to go.

Fail to model the culture and your employees will question your commitment to the cause and find it impossible to stay committed as well. At any given time, any given employee ought to be able to stand up for, market, or defend the company. You want that employee to have an unwavering view of the company's commitment to its mission and the cause. Model the culture yourself and that employee will be able to boldly state your mission, defend the institution, or challenge others who do not—without hesitation.

■ PRACTITIONER'S TIP
Model the culture.

Get input from wherever you can: from employees, customers, your management team, your board, and anyone you can talk into giving you an opinion. We say "talk into" because seeking out input is not as easy as it sounds. Most customers would prefer to vote with their feet (by walking away) than tell you they're unhappy. Those who do complain are doing you a great favor.

Similarly, many employees will not necessarily provide this feedback in the format *you* would prefer, such as standing up in your monthly meetings and saying what is on their minds. Provide them other opportunities to communicate their views, such as suggestion boxes or slips of paper prior to meetings to write anonymous questions and comments. And pay attention to nonformal communication such as the chatter in the lunchroom, the production numbers, staff turnover, and body language as you walk through the facility.

Pay particular attention to creating a safe way for your management team members to say what's on their minds. Consider using a "360-degree" review process, including all stakeholders, to provide feedback on the effectiveness of your leadership and management styles.

But in all of this, make one very important distinction. Ask for feedback, but never cede your obligation to be the place where the buck stops. Listen to everyone, discern, and then in the lonely solitude that you have the privilege and the responsibility to share only with yourself, make the best decisions you possibly can.

■ PRACTITIONER'S TIP
Seek feedback.

There's a funny thing about creating or running a social enterprise: it will change you more than you will change it. That's what happens when the common good gets in your blood.

It's what happened to Judy Wicks, of the White Dog Cafe fame. She would be the first to admit that she had no real grand vision. She started out as just a little muffin and coffee take-out shop. She got into the restaurant business as a waitress and had become the general manager of a place up the street and then a partner in it, but she was forced out by her partner because she was beginning to see it as a vehicle for progressive social change and he didn't. She started the White Dog on the first floor of her house because she wanted to express her own values and her own ideas about what business should be. But, she's quick to point out,

> I didn't really know terms like "socially responsible business," or "fair trade," or "living wage" or any of those things back then. My main thing was that I wanted to have

a community-based business that served my community and was a place where people could get healthy, local food and discuss the issues of the day. My mission just kind of developed more over time. My business will be twenty-five years old in January [2008], so I was a mere kid back then. And really, it was the kind of thing that evolved as I evolved, and I evolved because the business evolved. We kind of coevolved.[5]

Judy's comment was echoed by virtually everyone we interviewed in the writing of this book and certainly by the authors ourselves. Walls is fond of pointing new hires to the first line of Greyston's mission statement, which states, "Greyston Bakery is a force for personal transformation." It's a line that is as true for a brand-new employee as it is for Walls himself. The same sense of self-transformation is part of what Rebuild calls its Twelve Values, which speak of gaining greater self-worth, developing self-understanding and a sense of reality, achieving balance, and building strength and trust.

We are not the same individuals who arrived at Rebuild and Greyston five and twelve years ago, respectively. We believe, and hope that others have noticed as well, that we have continued to evolve into more spiritual, compassionate, intelligent, and less judgmental human beings.

Your role at the head of a social enterprise will almost certainly be a force for personal transformation, as it was for us, and as goes the story that is repeated over and over again by our fellow practitioners. Depending on your starting point, it will also undoubtedly round out your professional bag of tricks. By the time all is said and done you'll achieve familiarity with, if not downright mastery of, a whole host of previously unfamiliar skills.

Your journey will not be unlike our journeys have been. We've learned to add human relations and work skills where we were once able to get things done by sheer force of personality. We've advanced our financial skills and become comfortable at a more sophisticated level of management. We've worked on our weak spots and become even better at our strong suits. We've developed strong teams of managers who have increased the intellectual capacity of the organization way beyond our own. They've pushed us to advance our own skill sets to a more visionary and strategic perspective. Where once we were concerned about what was happening hour to hour, we've been able to shift our perspectives to day to day, then month to month, and when we're at the top of our games, to year to year.

We hope to keep changing, and we hope you'll do the same.

■ PRACTITIONER'S TIP
Coevolve.

It is a great privilege to lead a social enterprise. There is no other job to which you could aspire where you are given a goal as monumental as creating the common good and a tool as powerful as business for achieving that goal.

Respond to this privilege with awe, with wonder, and with gratitude. Approach it with the knowledge that it will take every ounce of skill, energy, and character you possess to lead it effectively. Even so, remember that if your enterprise succeeds, it will be because of others, and if it fails, it's not all about you.

To successfully lead your enterprise, you will be required to put every God-given talent you possess at the service of the common good, and you will discover capacities you never even knew you had been given. But never, *ever* fall into the trap of believing your own press. Never fail to consider the *source* of your giftedness.

■ **PRACTITIONER'S TIP**
Practice humility.

Take care of yourself. Then *let go* of self. And let the enterprise fly!

Epilogue

We're in a race. Can we social enterprisers, all together, make enough progress to turn enough things around, fast enough, to make a difference in the way things are headed?

We have to. And we can. If we remember the key words: "all together."

In no other field of endeavor have we witnessed the remarkable sense of cooperation that characterizes this world of social enterprise. All across the globe, forums, conferences, Listserv groups, publications, blogs, and endless other spaces are springing up where social enterprises freely share what they have learned with others. It is as though each of us belongs to an entire open-sourced industry that is growing at blazing speed.

We are trying to create a common good that is threatened by the competitive hunger of business as commonly practiced. Cooperation with each other is our hope and our secret weapon. It is the one strategy that traditional business is constitutionally incapable of practicing, co-opting, or adapting to.

It works because the common good builds on itself. Healthy people create healthy communities. Healthy communities protect healthy environments. Healthy environments foster healthy people. And the circle continues.

We are deeply appreciative of the wonderful social enterprise colleagues who shared their insights for this book. We are better practitioners after writing this book than we were when we started. We have learned from our colleagues just as we hope you will in turn learn and then teach others.

At times in your journey you will feel that you have nowhere to turn for counsel—lonely moments when the issues at hand will require measures of sensitivity, wisdom, judgment, and courage that are not available from your staff, your board, your friends, or your family. It will be in those instances that you can seek out a fellow social enterpriser.

In fact, that's how this book came about in the first place. For years, long before a book ever dawned on us, we would call each other whenever we needed advice or faced a struggle. Never did we fail to hear exactly the point of view we needed to hear and proceed with confidence toward a better outcome. We never would have become coauthors if we hadn't first become friends and co-mentors.

It is in this same spirit that we offer ourselves to you, for we can keep what we have been so freely given only by giving it away. Drop us an e-mail or give us a call if there's ever anything we can do to help *you* create the common good. We'll be sure to do the same.

Kevin Lynch, MissionIncLynch@gmail.com,
(612) 723-4209

Julius Walls, Jr., Julius@DoGoodDoWell.com,
(914) 882-1627

Contacts

To reach the Bainbridge Graduate Institute's magnificent Sustainable Business MBA candidates who were so instrumental in the development of this book, drop them an e-mail at the following addresses:

Linda Glasier, mutsi40@hotmail.com

Michael O'Brien, irishelement@hotmail.com

Paige Coleman, p.coleman@earthlink.net

Robert Marino, robertoberon@gmail.com

To learn more about any of the social enterprises described in this book (or to check out their wonderful products and services), visit the web sites below:

Benetech, http://www.benetech.org

Calvert Foundation, http://www.calvertfoundation.org

Community Wealth Ventures, http://www.community wealth.org

The Enterprising Kitchen, http://www.theenterprising kitchen.org

Evergreen Lodge, http://www.evergreenlodge.com

Give Something Back, http://www.givesomethingback.com

Good Capital, http://www.goodcap.net

Greyston Bakery, http://www.greystonbakery.com

Guayaki Yerba Mate, http://www.guayaki.com

Immaculate Baking Company, http://www.immaculate
baking.com

Indigenous Designs, http://www.indigenousdesigns.com

KaBOOM!, http://www.kaboom.org

The Kaleel Jamison Consulting Group, http://www.kjcg.com

Mal Warwick Associates, http://www.malwarwick.com

Nonprofit Finance Fund, http://www.nonprofitfinance
fund.org

Perlman & Perlman, http://www.perlmanandperlman.com

Rebuild Resources, Inc., http://www.rebuildstore.com,
http://www.rebuildresources.com

REDF, http://www.redf.org

Rubicon Programs, Inc., http://www.rubiconprograms.org

Seventh Generation, http://www.seventhgeneration.com

TROSA, http://www.trosainc.org

White Dog Cafe, http://www.whitedog.com

Notes

Preface

1. Kevin Lynch's friend Dan Wallace coined this phrase over coffee with him one day.

Introduction

1. Jerry Mander, *Four Arguments for the* Elimination *of Television* (New York: Quill, 1978), 127–128.
2. Marjorie Kelly, *The Divine Right of Capital: Dethroning the Corporate Aristocracy* (San Francisco: Berrett-Koehler, 2001), 5.
3. *Dictionary.com Unabridged (v 1.1)*, s.v. "Social," http:// dictionary.reference.com/browse/social (accessed April 19, 2007).
4. Wikipedia, s.v. "Social Enterprise," http://en.wikipedia.org/ wiki/Social_enterprise (access April 19, 2007).
5. Social Enterprise Alliance, "Social Enterprise Lexicon," http:// www.se-alliance.org/resources_lexicon.cfm.
6. Social Enterprise Reporter, http://www.sereporter.com/faq .php#definition.
7. Social Enterprise Coalition, "Social Enterprise Definitions," http://www.socialenterprise.org.uk/Page.aspx?SP=1878.
8. Jed Emerson and Fay Twersky, eds., *New Social Entrepreneurs: The Success, Challenge and Lessons of Non-profit Enterprise Creation* (San Francisco: The Roberts Foundation Homeless Economic Development Fund, 1996).
9. Nicole Etchart and Lee Davis, "Unique and Universal: Lessons from the Emerging Field of Social Enterprise in Emerging Market Countries" (a paper prepared for the Alcoa Foundation's Social Venture/Enterprise Initiative International Forum, Racine, WI, June 19–21, 2003), http://www.nesst.hu/ documents/NESsTUniqueandUniversalpaperMay2003.pdf.
10. Johnson Center at Grand Valley State University, "Nonprofit Good Practice Guide," http://www.npgoodpractice.org/ Glossary/Default.aspx?index=S.

11. Kim Alter, "Social Enterprise Typology," Virtue Ventures, LLC, 2007, http://www.virtueventures.com/setypology/index .php?id= DEFINITION&lm=1.
12. Manuel Velasquez, et al., "The Common Good," *Issues in Ethics 5*, no. 2 (Spring 1992).

Chapter 1
1. Rick Aubry, interview by Bainbridge Graduate Institute research team, April 2007.
2. Kevin McDonald, interview by Bainbridge Graduate Institute research team, May 2007.
3. Aubry interview.
4. Jeffrey Hollender, interview by Bainbridge Graduate Institute research team, April 2007.
5. Ibid.

Chapter 2
1. Shari Berenbach, interview by Bainbridge Graduate Institute research team, May 2007.
2. Joan Pikas, interview by Bainbridge Graduate Institute research team, May 2007.
3. Hollender interview.

Chapter 3
1. Social enterprise landscape chart and related discussion adapted from Mal Warwick, "Who Are You Calling a 'Social Enterprise'?," *Social Enterprise Reporter*, September 26, 2006.
2. Lee Zimmerman, interview by Bainbridge Graduate Institute research team, April 2007.
3. Kevin Jones, interview by Bainbridge Graduate Institute research team, April 2007.
4. Jim Fruchterman, interview by Bainbridge Graduate Institute research team, May 2007.
5. Clara Miller, interview by Bainbridge Graduate Institute research team, April 2007.

Chapter 4
1. Alan Lakein, "Alan Lakein Quotes," ThinkExist.com, http://thinkexist.com/quotes/alan_lakein/.
2. This quote is attributed to many including Napoleon and Field Marshall Von Molte.
3. From his song, "Beautiful Boy (Darling Boy)."

Chapter 5

1. Fruchterman interview.
2. McDonald interview.
3. Mike Hannigan, interview by Bainbridge Graduate Institute research team, May 2007.
4. Berenbach interview.
5. Clara Miller interview.

Chapter 6

1. Clara Miller interview.
2. Hollender interview.
3. Hannigan interview.
4. Darell Hammond, interview by Bainbridge Graduate Institute research team, May 2007.
5. Hannigan interview.
6. Ibid.
7. According to Amazon.com, "cultural creative" is a term coined by Paul Ray and Sherry Anderson "to describe people whose values embrace a curiosity and concern for the world, its ecosystem, and its peoples; an awareness of and activism for peace and social justice; and an openness to self-actualization through spirituality, psychotherapy, and holistic practices." See Paul H. Ray and Sherry Ruth Anderson, *The Cultural Creatives: How 50 Million People Are Changing the World* (New York: Three Rivers Press, 2001). LOHAS is an acronym for lifestyles of health and sustainability, a market segment focused on health and fitness, the environment, personal development, sustainable living, and social justice. See www .lohas.com.
8. Alfred Wise, interview by Bainbridge Graduate Institute research team, May 2007.
9. Chris Mann, interview by Bainbridge Graduate Institute research team, April 2007.
10. McDonald interview.
11. Fred Miller, interview by Bainbridge Graduate Institute research team, April 2007.
12. Mann interview.
13. Fred Miller interview.
14. Hammond interview.
15. McDonald interview.

Chapter 7

1. Jones interview.
2. Aubry interview.
3. Ibid.
4. Hannigan interview.
5. Hammond interview.
6. Hannigan interview.
7. Judy Wicks, interview by Bainbridge Graduate Institute research team, May 2007.
8. Hammond interview.
9. Scott Blackwell, interview by Bainbridge Graduate Institute research team, April 2007.
10. McDonald interview.
11. Zimmerman interview.

Chapter 8

1. Kelly, *The Divine Right of Capital*, quoting David C. Korten, "A New Focus: Corporate Cost Internalization," *Business Ethics* (July–August 1997): 16.
2. James P. Womack and Daniel T. Jones, *Lean Thinking* (New York: Simon & Schuster, 1996).
3. Masaaki Imai, *Kaizen: The Key to Japan's Competitive Success* (New York: McGraw Hill, 1986).
4. Hammond interview.

Chapter 9

1. Cynthia Gair, interview by Bainbridge Graduate Institute research team, May 2007.
2. Hannigan interview.
3. Hollender interview.
4. Ibid.
5. Fruchterman interview.
6. Ibid.
7. Hammond interview.
8. Mann interview.
9. McDonald interview.
10. Berenbach interview.
11. Aubry interview.
12. McDonald interview.
13. Gair interview.

14. Hammond interview.
15. Pikas interview.

Chapter 10

1. Clara Miller interview.
2. Aubry interview.
3. Scott Leonard, interview by Bainbridge Graduate Institute research team, May 2007.
4. Pikas interview.

Chapter 11

1. The Schwab Foundation for Social Entrepreneurship, "What Is a Social Entrepreneur?" http://www.schwabfound.org/whatis .htm.
2. McDonald interview.
3. Hollender interview.
4. McDonald interview.
5. Wicks interview.

Index

About Social Venture Network

SVN transforms the way the world does business by connecting, leveraging, and promoting a global community of leaders for a more just and sustainable economy.

Since its founding in 1987, SVN has grown from a handful of visionary individuals into a vibrant community of five hundred business owners, investors, and nonprofit leaders who are advancing the movement for social responsibility in business. SVN members believe in a new bottom line for business, one that values healthy communities and the human spirit as well as high returns.

As a network, SVN facilitates partnerships, strategic alliances, and other ventures that promote social and economic justice. SVN collects and promotes best practices for socially responsible enterprises and produces unique conferences that support the professional and personal development of business leaders and social entrepreneurs.

Please visit www.svn.org for more information on SVN membership, initiatives, and events.

About the Authors

Kevin Lynch is president of Rebuild Resources, Inc., a $2.2 million nonprofit social-purpose business in St. Paul, Minnesota, that helps chronic addicts and alcoholics find a path to sobriety through a program of spiritual recovery and work. Rebuild's business operations include a custom apparel and promotional-items business and a contract manufacturer. These businesses provide the recovery environment for Rebuild's student-employees and serve as the economic engines that fuel the enterprise.

Lynch is currently a board member of the Social Enterprise Alliance and has served on several national and local boards, including those of Social Venture Network, Headwaters Foundation for Justice, Twin Cities Community Gospel Choir, and (as the cofounder) Responsible Minnesota Business.

After starting and selling a direct mail business in college, Lynch spent twenty-one years in the advertising industry, the last fourteen as founder and principal of Lynch Jarvis Jones, a social enterprise ad agency whose mission was to create positive social change through the power of advertising and marketing. In early 2001, a series of synchronicities convinced him it was time to move on from the agency. He went on a two-year sabbatical, wherein he took a five-hundred-mile walk across Spain, shot photos, sang daily, learned a new language, served the peace movement, and, on the ninth anniversary of his own sobriety, stumbled into his current position at Rebuild.

Julius Walls, Jr., is CEO of Greyston Bakery and senior vice president of Greyston Foundation. Walls is also an adjunct professor at New York University's Stern School of Business, where he teaches social enterprise, and at Bainbridge Graduate Institute near Seattle, where he teaches social justice and business.

Born in Brooklyn, New York, Walls attended high school and college seminary before pursuing a career in business. He studied business at Baruch College and completed his degree at Concordia College. After beginning his career at an accounting firm, he joined a chocolate manufacturing company and at age twenty-six was appointed vice president of operations of the $23 million company. In 1992, he founded his own chocolate company, Sweet Roots, Inc., which sells the only chocolate bar using exclusively African cocoa and produced by an African-American.

Walls worked with Greyston Bakery to bring its cakes and tarts to the White House in 1993. In 1995, he joined Greyston as a marketing consultant and in November 1997 became CEO of the Bakery, adding vice president of Greyston Foundation in January 2000. A core ingredient of Walls's life and career is his spiritual practice. He encourages employees to actively bring their whole selves to work, including their cultural and spiritual selves. He has spoken extensively throughout the country on the topics of social ventures, social purpose businesses, spirituality in the workplace, and business development in the inner city. He is active in service to the community, serving on eight local and national boards. Walls resides in Yonkers with his wife, Cheryl, and three children.

Other Titles in the Social Venture Network Series

Values-Driven Business
How to Change the World, Make Money, and Have Fun
Ben Cohen and Mal Warwick

Written by high-profile entrepreneurs Ben Cohen (cofounder of Ben & Jerry's) and Mal Warwick, this engaging, accessible guide points the way to a new, socially responsible business ethic and offers entrepreneurs and owners the practical tools they need to embed their values in their businesses.

$14.95, paperback, 192 pages, ISBN 978-1-57675-358-3

True to Yourself
Leading a Values-Based Business
Mark Albion

From the author of the *New York Times* bestseller *Making a Life, Making a Living* comes the ultimate leadership guide for socially responsible small businesses and entrepreneurs.

$14.95, paperback, 192 pages, ISBN 978-1-57675-378-1

Marketing That Matters
10 Practices to Profit Your Business and Change the World
Chip Conley and Eric Friedenwald-Fishman

Award-winning marketers Chip Conley and Eric Friedenwald-Fishman prove that "marketing" is not a dirty word—instead, it's key to advancing both the value and values of any business. They offer a thorough and practical guide to selling what you do without selling out who you are.

$14.95, paperback, 216 pages, ISBN 978-1-57675-383-5

Growing Local Value
How to Build Business Partnerships That Strengthen Your Community
Laury Hammel and Gun Denhart

Hanna Andersson founder Gun Denhart and BALLE cofounder Laury Hammel show how every aspect of a business (from product creation to employee recruitment to vendor selection) holds the dual promise of bigger profits and a stronger local community.

$14.95, paperback, 192 pages, ISBN 978-1-57675-371-2

Values Sell
Transforming Purpose into Profit Through Creative Sales and Distribution Strategies
Nadine A. Thompson and Angela E. Soper

In this practical and inspiring guide, Nadine Thompson and Angela Soper draw on real-world examples to detail concrete steps for designing sales and distribution strategies that fit the needs, habits, and interests of your target customers. They show how to turn your stakeholders into enthusiastic partners by ensuring that all your relationships—with your salespeople as well as other employees, your customers, and your suppliers—are beneficial and fulfilling on more than just an economic level.

$14.95, paperback, 192 pages, ISBN 978-1-57675-421-4

BE CONNECTED

Visit Our Website

Go to www.bkconnection.com to read exclusive previews and excerpts of new books, find detailed information on all Berrett-Koehler titles and authors, browse subject-area libraries of books, and get special discounts.

Subscribe to Our Free E-Newsletter

Be the first to hear about new publications, special discount offers, exclusive articles, news about bestsellers, and more! Get on the list for our free e-newsletter by going to www .bkconnection.com.

Get Quantity Discounts

Berrett-Koehler books are available at quantity discounts for orders of ten or more copies. Please call us toll-free at (800) 929-2929 or email us at bkp.orders@aidcvt.com.

Host a Reading Group

For tips on how to form and carry on a book reading group in your workplace or community, see our website at www .bkconnection.com.

Join the BK Community

Thousands of readers of our books have become part of the "BK Community" by participating in events featuring our authors, reviewing draft manuscripts of forthcoming books, spreading the word about their favorite books, and supporting our publishing program in other ways. If you would like to join the BK Community, please contact us at bkcommunity@ bkpub.com.